So Devon

Brian Le Messurier

Brian Le Messurier has lived in Devon for 59 years, and has written eight books about the West Country, and collaborated with other writers on several more.

He is a qualified Blue Badge Tourist Guide, and before retirement worked for the National Trust as a Countryside Interpretation Officer.

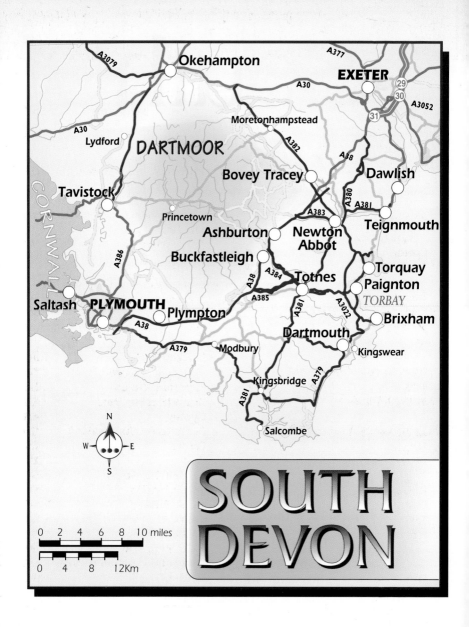

SOUTH DEVON

Acknowledgements:
Original maps for the cartography supplied by Michael Bell of Bells
Books, Halifax Tel: 01422 365468

CONTENTS

• AUTHOR'S FAVOURITES •

Here, in no particular order, are the places in this area of South Devon that the author feels are rather special.

Exeter Cathedral (page 20)

Stands out as the finest building — secular or ecclesiastical — in the West Country

Totnes (page 42)

One of Britain's top forty towns for its wealth of historic interest. Has a castle, good church and town walls — and much besides

Tavistock (page 63)

A highly attractive town, well-sited by the river Tavy, good for shopping and with relics of Tavistock Abbey dotted about

Plymouth Hoe (page 56)

Along with the Thames at London and Dover Strait, the most evocative maritime landscape and viewpoint in Great Britain

Lydford Gorge (page 73)

A frighteningly deep and awesome natural river gorge. The nearby castle and fossilised Saxon village site also should be visited

Castle Drogo (page 77)

A twentieth-century, granite country house, impressively built on a spur looking towards Dartmoor. Excellent views, good gardens

Morwellham (page 65)

The revitalised Tamar-side port at the terminus of the Tavistock Canal. A great day out, with underground tram rides in the mines

The coastline around Salcombe (page 48)

Accessible by the coast path and especially beautiful and unspoilt between Bolt Tail and Start Point

• BEACHES •

Exeter to Teignmouth

Safe, sandy beaches can be found at Dawlish Warren, Dawlish and Teignmouth.

Torbay

Torquay's success as a holiday resort has been achieved despite not having any large beaches. Torre Abbey Sands are mostly covered at high tide, and the other opportunities to enjoy the seaside are at Meadfoot Beach, Anstey's Cove and Oddicombe, where a cliff railway assists visitors to reach the shore.

Slapton Sands

Petitor is the unofficial naturist beach.

It was Paignton which developed as the family resort and remains so to this day, with better sandy beaches, both off the promenade and at Goodrington. Between Paignton and Brixham is Broadsands, a safe, sandy beach where dogs are banned.

Brixham only has very small beaches, a mixture of shingle and sand, at Churston Cove and Fishcombe.

There is limited surfing at Hollicombe Beach and Preston Beach.

Dartmouth to Salcombe

Blackpool Sands near Stoke Fleming is a safe swimming beach but the name is a misnomer as there is more shingle than sand. Dogs are banned here. The long stretch of Slapton Sands, mainly shingle, past Torcross is not recommended for swimming but is excellent for walking.

Salcombe has two safe, sandy beaches, North Sands (with the remains of one of Henry VIII's castles on one of its promontories; it withstood a siege in the Civil War) and South Sands. Dogs are banned from the latter.

Salcombe to Plymouth

Thurlestone and South Milton Sands offer excellent opportunities for windsurfers. Further along, Bigbury, with its access to Burgh Island, is safe and sandy as is nearby Challaborough which is also dog free. Nearer to Plymouth there are few opportunities for safe swimming but Mothecombe, Wembury and Bovisand all offer pleasant pottering and sunbathing.

Devon is an enormous county, as wide north to south as Cornwall is long east to west, and it can be broken up into several parts for the purpose of guide book writing.

North Devon, that part of the county north of Dartmoor, separates off neatly, as does East Devon, the area between the Exe estuary and the Dorset boundary, leaving Exeter as the county town — though it is in fact a city — to act as a the gateway to South Devon and Dartmoor.

The appearance of Devon is due to physical and historical accidents. A geological movement millions of years ago so tilted the south-west peninsula that the long rivers run north to south and the high ground of Dartmoor is on the northern part of the moor.

The estuaries of the south-flowing rivers created an indented coastline which was good for harbours — one thinks of Plymouth, Teignmouth and Dartmouth. These ports became important during the years of warfare between England and its historical enemies, France and Spain, and 160 years ago the main railway line to Cornwall was routed through South Devon, rather than further north, to link up these settlements and others.

The wild upland of Dartmoor, since 1951 a National Park, is very different from cosy lowland Devon. Altitude, exposure, geology and soil have all contributed to this, so that in this book we are considering three types of landscape outside the urban areas — coastal scenery, pastoral countryside and rough moorland.

Early Settlements

The visitor wishing to see how early man lived in Devon is advised to head for Dartmoor with a detailed Ordnance Survey map and search out the stone remains of his houses and ritual monuments. These have survived because of the hard granite of which they were made and the lack of subsequent disturbance. The ruined foundations of the Bronze Age (say 1500BC) dwellings are the most abundant and evocative of these antiquities. They are shown as 'hut circles' on maps.

Hill forts — sometimes confusingly called 'castles' but lacking medieval masonry — came later and suggest that the cult of the tribe was well developed and that the people were warlike.

The Romans established a base at Exeter and sent out tentative probes beyond rather like the cavalry on the North American plains in the early nineteenth century. The most spectacular of the post-war archaeological digs in the city uncovered a legionary bath-house, which had to be backfilled after excavation.

Dark Ages

After the withdrawal of the Romans we enter the Dark Ages, those mysterious centuries whose enigmatic annals seem lost for ever.

To fill the vacuum, and on the slenderest evidence, commentators have created the Arthurian legends, but they apply to Cornwall and Somerset rather than to Devon. The Saxons gradually pushed westwards and King Alfred began to put the defences of Wessex in order but the Danes kept niggling away with raids inland from their longships.

Rougemont Castle

Exeter capitulated with honour to King William two years after the Battle of Hastings but he was determined to show the ordinary citizens that the Normans were the conquerors and built Rougemont Castle on the highest part of Exeter's walls. These were originally laid out by the Romans and, much patched up, are still visible today.

It is an interesting fact that after over 900 years the tradition of law and order is still upheld from the castle. Exeter Crown Court meets in eighteenth-century buildings within its precincts and indeed the ordinary people of Exeter regard the castle with something akin to awe and only venture within its walls, whether as witnesses or jurors, with reluctance. A long-standing folk memory perhaps?

Medieval Devon

Then began the true documentary history of Devon. The *Domesday Book,* a kind of natural census, was compiled and for the first time we know the structure of society in England.

Much of the early history of Devon is bound up with that of Exeter and so the trend continued. Plymouth, by far the largest place in present-day Devon, is not mentioned in records until 1211. Devon's history in medieval times was punctuated by the departures for the Crusades and the arrival of the Black Death. Later, the pretender Perkin Warbeck and the Prayer Book Rebellion passed through the county.

Armada to Waterloo

The scene now shifts to Plymouth and the sea. Sir Francis Drake and Sir John Hawkins both lived nearby, and it is said that the Armada was first sighted in Devon from the cliffs near Hope Cove.

In the middle of the seventeenth century the Civil War ebbed and flowed across the land. In 1688 William of Orange landed at Brixham with a vast army, many of them continental mercenaries. James II was ousted and William and Mary took the throne.

For half of the following 127 years, until Waterloo, England was at war with France. Plymouth developed as a naval base, but trade was thwarted and foreign trade inhibited. Road transport

Ashprington village with the Waterman's Arms visible through the branches on the left

was encouraged by the first of the Devon Turnpike Acts in 1753. Roads were improved and stage-coaches began to make road travel easier and more reliable.

Growth of Torquay

The British fleet, finding that it could very easily be bottled up at Plymouth, began to use the sheltered waters of Tor Bay as an anchorage until Plymouth Break-water was built, well into the nineteenth century.

It was the fleet medical officers, understanding the climatic bene-fits of the area, who began to recommend Torquay to their consumptive patients. Thus it was as a haven for invalids that the village of Torquay became a town and later, a holiday resort. In the 1840s the railway reached Devon and the chosen route soon established the holiday resorts, although widespread car owner-ship has made many people independent of the railways.

20th Century South Devon

World War I had little effect on Devon, except to cream off the pride of its men-folk, as a glance at any war memorial will show. In World War II the battle came to Devon. Exeter and Plymouth were blitzed out of all recognition and Teignmouth and Exmouth were also badly damaged. Slap-ton Sands was used by the US forces for invasion exercises in 1943 and seven parishes in the hinterland were evacuated as live ammunition was used.

In the years since the war the railways have contracted, the dual carriageways and M5 motor-way have arrived, caravan and camping sites have multiplied and sailing and self-catering holi-days are in vogue. Devon is now competing with cheap overseas package tours but because of its heritage of history and beauty, its accessibility and hospitality, there is an enormous amount to see and do in the county.

Here are just a few suggestions for walks along the coast, all of which use parts of the South West Coast Path. They are not intended as detailed routes but suggestions which can be used and adapted with the aid of the appropriate OS map. Stout shoes or walking boots are advisable and a drink and some food should be carried on the longer walks.

Shaldon to Torquay

That part of the South West Coast Path between Shaldon and Torquay makes a very good day's walk. As it cuts across the grain of the landscape, it is a strenuous expedition, but may be shortened at several places by turning off the coast path to the A379 for a bus back to Shaldon or Torquay. Details of bus services and linked walks can be found in *The Smugglers' Trail,* a leaflet published by Stagecoach Devon (☎ 01803 613226).

Berry Head to Kingswear

A good walk from Berry Head is to follow the cliff path to Kingswear, returning to Brixham by bus. Four hours are needed for the 10 miles (16km) of strenuous walking and there are no pick-up points along the way. Alternatively take the bus to Kingswear and walk back to Berry Head, allowing time at the end of the day to enjoy the pleasures of the country park there.

Little Dartmouth to Gallants Bower

A shorter walk reveals views of the coast south of Dartmouth. From the National Trust car park at Little Dartmouth near Stoke Fleming one can walk to Gallants Bower, above Dartmouth Castle and return by way of the coast path with views ahead across Start Bay to Start Point. This round trip of about 3 miles (5km) is delightfully varied and could perhaps include a picnic in the grounds of Dartmouth Castle.

Prawle Point to Gammon Head

This is also a short walk but could have the added enjoyment of a swim. A mile away by cliff path from Prawle Point south of Kingsbridge, is Gammon Head, the most

photogenic promontory on the South Devon coast. Its
massive hump protects a sheltered beach, Maceley Cove,
from the south-west gales, and is a lovely spot for a swim,
even if the climb down and up is rather a scramble. The
less energetic can sit and enjoy the views across the
estuary to Bolt Head and watch the comings and goings
from Salcombe Harbour.

Prawle Point to East Portlemouth

A further walk, from Prawle Point to East Portlemouth (on
the east side of Salcombe harbour, and linked to Salcombe
by foot ferry) and back, will take the best part of a day (a
round trip of about 12 miles (19km). On from the Gara
Rock Hotel there are alternative paths, low level and high
level, which could be used to vary the return route for part
of the way.

Overbecks circular walk

Visitors should on no account omit the walk up the steep
lane behind Overbecks just outside Salcombe. This is a
pleasant high-level path leading to a viewpoint indicator on
the top of Sharp Tor, overlooking Starehole Bay, the last
resting place of the four-masted Finnish barque the
Herzogin Cecilie, which was wrecked in 1936. Along this
high path, a steep path leads down to the back of the bay.
The return to Overbecks can be made along the lower path,
the Courtenay Walk, which cuts through the spiky rocks of
Sharp Tor, a round trip of 2 miles (3km).

Throughout South Devon there are lovely gardens, from the smallest cottages to stately homes, seafront gardens and flower beds adorning the many popular attractions in the area. There are some gardens, though, that should be visited for themselves, rather than as secondary to another attraction. These are a few suggestions.

Killerton

The gardens of Killerton House, owned by the National Trust, are a delight. Easily reached from Exeter, they can be found some 6 miles (9.5km) north-east of the City at Broadclyst. This beautiful hillside garden is a subtle blend of herbaceous borders, lawns, shrubs and trees, especially rhododendrons and magnolias. It also features an ice house and an early nineteenth-century rustic-style summer house known as the Bear Hut. There are walks in the surrounding parkland. Wheelchair access to parts of the garden. Tearoom and shop, although these will not be open every day in the winter. ☎ 01392 881345. Open: All year, 10.30am–dusk.

Coleton Fishacre Garden

Tucked in a small stream-fed valley leading down to the sea near the Day Mark, 3 miles (5km) south-east of Kingswear. This National Trust garden is a 15-acre (6 hectares) sub-tropical paradise only begun by the D'Oyly Carte family (of Gilbert and Sullivan fame) in the 1920s. It features a variety of rare and exotic shrubs and trees, with particularly fine autumn colours. Limited wheelchair access is possible but there are steep slopes to negotiate. Tea-garden, weather permitting. ☎ 01803 752466. Open March, Sundays only 2pm–5pm. April to end of October, Wednesday, Thursday, Friday, Sunday and Bank Holiday Mondays 10.30am– 5.30pm (dusk if earlier).

Overbecks Garden

Situated $1^1/_2$ miles (2.5km) south-west of Salcombe, the gardens at Overbecks Museum and Garden (National Trust) are an attraction in themselves. The micro-climate that exists here allows plants and shrubs to grow that one would not expect to find in England. The beautiful and luxuriant garden also enjoys spectacular views over the Salcombe estuary. Wheelchair access is possible but there are steep paths and some are gravel-surfaced. The tearoom and shop are only open between April and October on days when the Museum is open. ☎ 01548 842893. Garden open daily throughout the year, 10am–8pm or sunset if earlier.

The Garden House, Buckland Monachorum

About 3 miles (5km) west of Yelverton, a little way north of Buckland Abbey, the Garden House has a magnificent 8 acre (3 hectares) garden, one of the best in the county. This is very much a 'gardener's garden' with many unusual plants. Tearoom. ☎ 01822 854769. Open: March to October, daily 10.30am–5pm.

Lukesland Gardens

Just to the north of Ivybridge ($1^1/_4$ miles (2km)) at Harford, the Lukesland Gardens are 15 acres (6 hectares) of woodland and garden, with landscaped pools and waterfalls. The rhododendrons and azaleas are the highlight of this magnificent site. ☎ 01752 893390. Open: Mid-April to Mid-June Sundays, Wednesdays and Bank Holidays 2–6pm.

• EXETER •

Taking the broad view, one of the appealing aspects of Exeter is its size; large enough to attract specialised shops, events and institutions, but small enough to be comfortably cosy.

Looking down the main street there are green fields only a couple of miles away. From the highest part of the city, Pennsylvania (the 1822 builder of Pennsylvania Park was a Quaker who named his terrace after the American province) and from the Exeter Bypass, the sea and the super-tankers off Torbay can be seen due south; Dartmoor is visible due west.

Exeter's old buildings, the Cathedral and the Guildhall apart, do not make a great impact, and many of the more interesting features of its heritage have to be searched for. On a dull or wet day in August, when tourists swarm to the city and the car parks show 'Full' signs, the Cathedral Close and High Street teem with life.

Sadly few day visitors penetrate to Rougemont Gardens below the castle, walk the line of the city walls, or visit the under-ground passages. The latter are, in fact, misnamed. While appearing to be just that, they were built in the fourteenth and fifteenth centuries to bring water into the city from springs outside the walls.

Underground Passages

Romangate Passage, off High Street. Exhibition and video presentation followed by guided tour of the medieval aqueducts. Unsuitable for wheelchairs and sufferers from claustrophobia. ☎ 01392 265887. Open: July to September and school holidays, Monday to Saturday 10am–5.30pm. Rest of the year, Tuesday to Friday 2–5pm and Saturday 10am–5pm. Last tour 45mins before closing.

Town Centre Tour

Since so much of old Exeter was destroyed in May 1942, the remaining historic buildings and places of interest are slightly off-centre, and can best be linked by a walk round the walls, with a deflection here and there to see something near at hand.

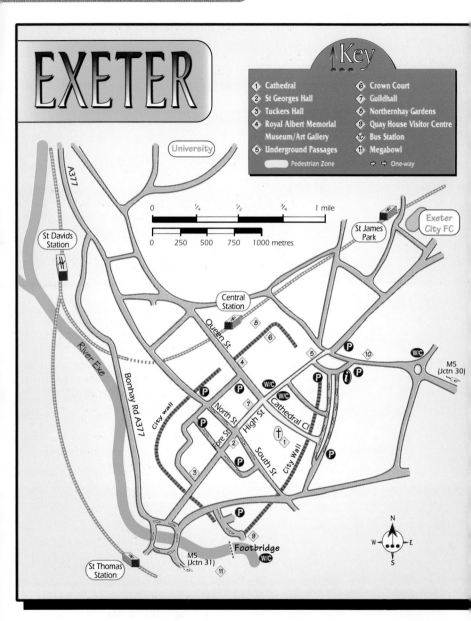

EXETER

Key

1. Cathedral
2. St Georges Hall
3. Tuckers Hall
4. Royal Albert Memorial Museum/Art Gallery
5. Underground Passages
6. Crown Court
7. Guildhall
8. Northernhay Gardens
9. Quay House Visitor Centre
10. Bus Station
11. Megabowl

Pedestrian Zone
One-way

Visitors are always surprised at the variety of interest which lies between the ancient core and the newer Exeter outside the walls. The distance is 2,600yd (2,377m) and the area enclosed is 93 acres (37 hectares). Five-sixths of the city wall is still visible and the walk round the complete circuit takes between $1\frac{1}{2}$ and 2 hours.

A good place to start is opposite Boots the Chemists, where a line of paving slabs, laid as broken pieces, marks a length of the **city wall** where it has disappeared. Although it can be followed in either direction, as one way seems to go through the front door of Boots, the other may be more fruitful! At once a corner bastion may be seen; a wall plaque states that the city walls were originally built by the Romans about AD200 and they have since been rebuilt and restored after every siege.

As the wall is followed, at Bedford Street one enters Southernhay East where, on one of Exeter's elegant Georgian terraces, are some curious Coade stone keystones of moulded faces. Turn behind No 9 to rediscover the wall and follow it to South Street where two more wall plaques, one on either side of the street, explain that the massive **South Gate**, demolished in 1819, was for many years a prison.

From here it is worth deviating along Magdalen Street to see **Wynard's Almshouses**, opposite the one-time Eye Infirmary. Round a cobbled courtyard, still with its well-head, is a pleasing group of red sandstone cottages and a chapel. Founded in the fifteenth century and rebuilt several times since, the buildings were converted into offices for various voluntary organisations in the 1970s.

Now return to the site of South Gate and cross Western Way at the traffic lights and follow the wall to the back of the **Custom House** (1681), the first building in Exeter to be constructed from brick in modern times, and the

Quay House Visitor Centre where the history of the city, particularly the river quays, is explored. This part of Exeter is also the heart of Exeter's nightlife, with discos and clubs accommodated in old warehouses.

Quay House Visitor Centre

The Quay. Free audio visual programme on the history of Exeter.
☎ 01392 265213.
Open: Easter to October, daily 10am–5pm.

Now resume the wall circuit. Behind the Custom House and along the rather down-at-heel alley, Cricklepit Street, on the left are the remains of Exeter's last **watermill**, with the skeleton of an undershot waterwheel. This mill was first recorded in 1190. On Western Way, across the road is a ruined church which stands on a bridge now high and dry. This was Exeter's first bridge (1240) and it crossed a much wider river. The Exe now runs in a narrower and deeper channel beyond.

Stepcote Hill, the cobbled medieval way into the city, climbs steeply up beside **St Mary Steps church**. Until 1778 this was the main road into Exeter from the west. The church has a famous clock, with various parts that can be seen to move when it strikes the hour. Facing it is a wooden-framed Tudor building known as 'The House that Moved'. In 1961 it was in the way of the new road, but by strapping it together and jacking it up on rollers the little building was moved to its present site and saved for posterity.

Walk up West Street to Fore Street, now the main way into Exeter from the west. The route is straight ahead up Bartholomew Street, but turn briefly up Fore Street for 50yd (46m), where on the left will be seen the Victorian façade of a 1471 building, the **Tucker's Hall**. Here the craft gild (*sic*) of the Exeter woollen trade, the weavers, fullers and shearmen met, and, in a somewhat altered form, still meet.

Tucker's Hall

140 Fore Street.
Medieval building with original roof timbers and Jacobean panelling. ☎ 01392 436244. Open: June to September, Tuesday, Thursday, Friday: October to May, Thursday, 10.30am–12.30pm.

St Nicholas Priory

The Mint, off Fore Lane. Norman undercroft and kitchen, Tudor room, medieval furniture and fittings. Open: Easter to end of October, Monday, Wednesday and Saturday, 3pm–4.30pm.

Return to the foot of Bartholemew Street and carry on up to a walk-way along the top of

the walls beside a restored chapel of 1817 with a Doric porch. This leads to a pleasant backwater known as Ash Grove where the wall turns 90 degrees right and follows along the top of the Long Brook Valley.

Where the path meets the road go through some iron gates on the left, and down some narrow steep steps to a lower level. Here one is standing outside the **Exeter catacombs**, built against the walls in the Egyptian style of 1811 then in vogue and operated in a desultory fashion until 1883. They never caught on as a way of disposing of the dead, and are now sealed off. The stacks of slate 'pigeon holes', some occupied, may be seen by peering through the grill.

A hundred yards away from the wall, is **St Nicholas Priory**, a well preserved part of a once much larger building with many Norman features. The guest hall on the first floor is a particularly handsome room.

The walk is resumed to the foot of North Street (traffic lights) where there was another gate, **North Gate**, and below one can see the **Iron Bridge**, an early example of cast-iron civil engineering. It was built to ease the approach to this side of Exeter for horse-drawn vehicles.

Up Northernhay Street, Queen Street contains some of Exeter's best nineteenth-century architecture. The classical **Higher Market** (1838, now adapted as a shopping precinct) and the **Royal Albert Memorial Museum** (1865-6) in Early English revival are worth seeing.

Royal Albert Memorial Museum

Queen Street. Wide ranging displays including silver, costume, paintings, flora and fauna. Temporary exhibitions throughout the year. Shop and café. Wheelchair access.
☎ 01392 265858.
Open: All year, Monday to Saturday, 10am–5pm.

Across Queen Street are Northernhay Gardens with the walls on the right. Head towards the Exeter War Memorial. An area laid out as a public space as long ago as 1612. A small door in the wall leads into Rougemont Gardens. At the far end of the gardens from the little door is the Regency building called Rougemont House, now home to the Connections Discovery Centre, a hands-on interpretation centre for schoolchildren.

Opposite is the gatehouse to the **castle**, now redundant, as the present-day entrance stands alongside. Inside the castle yard are the Palladian (1774) court buildings, but admission is granted only to those on business or jury service as the shell of William the Conqueror's castle now houses Exeter's Crown Court! One can leave the garden through Athelstan's Tower, an attractive viewpoint. Athelstan reigned

Left: Lammas Fair
Below: Quayside warehouses

from 925 to 940, and this tower is part of William's post-conquest fortifications.

Exeter Cathedral

To visit the **Cathedral** enter the Cathedral Close by Broadgate, where one of several gates into the Close stood in medieval times. The simple stone **Devon War Memorial** on the right, designed by Lutyens, stands on the site of the Roman bathhouse excavated in the early 1970s and now covered over.

The cathedral's twin towers are Norman, although perforated by later Gothic windows, and are all that survive of the cathedral built between 1133 and 1160. Bishop Bronescombe became dissatisfied with this building and began rebuilding it in 1270, but his conception was not completed for about a hundred years.

Inside, from beneath the west window is a good view of the 300ft (105m)-long unbroken tierceron vaulting. This weighs about 5,000 tons and stands on columns of Pur-beck (Dorset) stone. Much of the cathedral is of stone from Beer in East Devon.

The roof bosses have been restored to their original medieval colours. Churches in the Middle Ages were dazzlingly colourful, and where possible the brightness has been put back in Exeter Cathedral. Look especially for the complicated boss dating from 1350 in the second bay from the west, which depicts the murder of Archbishop Thomas Becket in Canterbury Cathedral in 1170.

Other glories to look for are the Minstrel Gallery of about the same date, the Bishop's Throne (1312-17) which is regarded as the finest piece of wood carving of its age in Europe, and the tombs in the colourful Lady Chapel at the east end.

The side chapel behind the throne, St James' Chapel, was destroyed by a bomb in World War II, but fortunately the throne had been taken to pieces and removed to the country for safety; otherwise it would have become so many wood splinters. Shrapnel damage can be seen above the choir. The chapel is now restored.

Of the buildings in **Cathedral Close** the most noteworthy is Mol's Coffee House, its bay windows a reminder of Drake and Hawkins when they met and chatted over their coffee. Though there is nothing else to match Mol's, taken together the Close's buildings comprise a delightful scene. It is here, in St Martin's Lane and along Gandy Street (the other side of High Street) that the essence of Exeter's attraction is most deeply felt.

The Guildhall

High Street, Exeter. The oldest municipal building in the country. Fifteenth-century arch-braced timber roof, standing behind a Tudor pillared front of 1592. ☎ 01392 265213. Open: (subject to civic functions) all year, Monday to Friday 10.30am–4.pm; Saturday 10.30am–12 noon.

Recent Developments

In recent years, three major developments have taken place to expand Exeter's sporting, leisure and artistic life.

The **Clifton Hill Sports Centre** offers facilities for badminton, basketball, keep fit, gymnastics, volley ball and more informal activities; the **Plaza Leisure Centre** offers squash, snooker, swimming, weight training and other special features; while the **Exeter and Devon Arts Centre** in Bradninch Place is the place to go if you are interested in dance, folk, jazz, rock, film, theatre or cabaret. Classes and courses are always on the go and there is a bar and café.

Exeter has sprawled east and south in living memory, gobbling up the villages of Heavitree, Whipton and Pinhoe, though the residents of Clyst St Mary might object to their village being called a part of Exeter. Here, at **Crealy Park**, is one of Devon's finest sites for children, with every conceivable ride (on land and water) as well as such favourites as a pets' corner.

i Crealy

Clyst St Mary, nr Exeter. Indoor and outdoor adventure playgrounds, Children's Village, rides. Restaurant and snack bar. Large gift and toy shop. ☎ 01395 233200. Open: April to October, daily, 10am–6pm; November to March 10.30am–5pm.

The Cathedral

• SOUTH-WEST OF EXETER •

As one travels south-west from Exeter the view is blocked by the Haldon Hills, a flint-topped plateau of greensand and sandstone, similar in many ways to the Devon hills inland from Sidmouth. Being flat-topped and not dipping below 600ft (210m) except in the saddle between Great and Little Haldon and with a modest maximum altitude of 826ft (289m), this range cries out for an artificial eye-catcher. One was provided in the late eighteenth century when Sir Robert Palk built the three-sided Lawrence Castle (often called Haldon Belvedere) on Penn Hill.

Powderham Castle, Exeter

The mouth of the estuary is marked by **Dawlish Warren**, a popular resort which has developed beside the sandspit which protrudes towards Exmouth. The plants and birdlife are of national importance, and there is a visitor centre open in the summer where information on the natural history of the area can be found.

Nearby lies **Powderham Castle**, the home of the Courtenay family, the Earls of Devon, since 1390, standing in one of the finest parks in the county. Perhaps the most interesting rooms in the house are the marble hall and the staircase hall. The former contains a 13ft (4.5m) longcase clock by Stumbels of Totnes (1740) which plays a tune at 4, 8 and 12 o'clock.

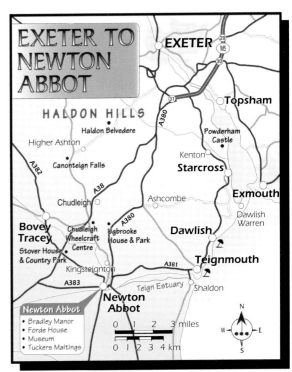

Powderham Castle

Kenton, near Exeter. The estate should be entered by the drive from Powderham village following the signs from Red Lodge. Amalgam of architectural styles. Events throughout the summer. Large herd of fallow deer. ☎ 01626 890243. Open: end of March to end of October, daily except Saturday, 10am–5.30pm. Grounds open from beginning of March.

Travelling west along the A380, a few miles further on the motorist will see a sign reading 'Ugbrooke House', the stately home and estate belonging to Lord Clifford, which sits retiringly in the quiet countryside between the A380 and the A38. The house dates for the most part from about 1750 when Robert Adam rebuilt the earlier Tudor manor house and Capability Brown landscaped the park.

However the house's recent history is equally interesting. In the 1930s the 11th Lord Clifford left Ugbrooke as he could not afford to live there, and during the war it became a school for evacuees and a hostel for Poles. In the 1950s several downstairs rooms, now beautifully restored, were used as grain stores. The present Lord and Lady Clifford returned from Australia in 1957, and began the enormous task of bringing life and beauty back into the house and park.

Ugbrooke House and Park

Chudleigh. Collection of paintings, dolls, furniture and military uniforms.
☎ 01626 852179. Open: Mid-July to early September, Tuesday to Thursday and Sunday; grounds 1-5.30pm; admission to the House by Guided Tours only, 2.00pm and 3.45pm.

A short distance from Ugbrooke is **Chudleigh,** once on the busy A38, but now bypassed by the dual carriageway to Plymouth. Much of medieval Chudleigh was destroyed in the great fire of 1807, when two-thirds of the town was burnt down.

At the foot of Clifford Street is the **Wheel Craft Centre,** occupying the old Town Mills. Here a number of different craftsmen go about their business on view to the public, and their products are on sale.

About 3 miles (5km) west of Chudleigh, is the **Canonteign Falls and Farm Park.** A natural hillside gorge was landscaped by the first Viscountess Exmouth 160 years ago. Water was fed to a cascade by a leat. After many years of neglect this beautiful corner of the Teign Valley has been restored and the paths cleared.

Canonteign Falls and Lakeland

On B3193, just off A38. Highest waterfall in England. Nature trails. Junior assault course. Tearoom and gift shop.
☎ 01647 252434. Open: Early March to mid-November, daily 10am–5.30pm. Winter opening: Sundays and school holidays, 11am–4pm.

the lake. A great deal of work was done a few years ago to make the park, which had become derelict, beautiful once again, and available to the public. Birds and dragonflies are present in abundance, and fishing can be tried from special platforms.

Close to the Park is **Orchid Paradise,** a superb orchid collection housed in a plant nursery. Also near the Park, Trago Mills is a shopping complex with a number of play areas for children.

Westwards from Chudleigh along the A38 for 3 miles (5km) as far as the Drum Bridge intersection, there is a left turn, signposted 'Newton Abbot', and almost immediately a left turn into **Stover Country Park,** managed by Devon County Council. There is a pleasant walk round

Orchid Paradise

Off A382 at Forches Cross. Artificial climate of all-year, sunny spring, houses large variety of orchids. Original gift ideas on an orchid theme.
☎ 01626 352233. Open: All year except winter bank holidays, daily 10am–4pm.

• NEWTON ABBOT AND DISTRICT •

Newton Abbot is at first sight an unprepossessing town. Its attractions have to be searched for, but many pleasant small buildings are waiting to be discovered.

St Leonard's Tower, Newton Abbot

The River Lemon passes through the built-up area and is largely culverted, a fact which fails to allow for the occasional flash-flood. The St Leonard's Tower, which stands at the central crossroads, is all that remains of a church built about 1350 and demolished in 1836.

Close to the town centre can be found **Tuckers Maltings**, the only traditional malthouse in the country which is open to the public.

Tuckers Maltings

Teign Road, Newton Abbot. Demonstration of 'Barley to Beer'. Discovery Centre. Shop. Light refreshments.
☎ 01626 334734.
Open: Good Friday to 31 October, daily from 10am. Guided tours lasting 1 hour, every 30–45 mins.

Two outstanding buildings are within easy reach of Newton Abbot centre, albeit in opposite directions. **Bradley Manor,** is a small fifteenth-century manor house standing in its own grounds. Its great hall, emblazoned with Queen Elizabeth's royal arms, is a notable feature. In the woods beyond Bradley Manor is Puritan Pit, a deep natural cavity where early nonconformists held their meetings in secret 300 years ago.

Bradley Manor (National Trust)

Totnes Road, Newton Abbot. No facilities. ☎ 01626 354513. Open: April to September, Wednesday 2–5pm. Also certain Thursdays 2–5pm.

At the other end of the town **Forde House,** now used by Teignbridge District Council, dates from 1610. King Charles I visited in 1625, and William of Orange read his proclamation here in 1688, on his way to London, after landing at Brixham. Viewing is by appointment only, ☎ 01626 361101.

'Racing at Newton Abbot' refers to the national hunt racecourse on the Kingsteignton road. During the rest of the year, it is used for stock car racing, greyhound racing and country shows.

A little way out, and beyond the large village of Ipplepen, is the parish of **Torbryan,** which should be visited for the sake of its church and the Church House Inn. This remote church — it stands at the end of a cul-de-sac — was never restored, and retains to a remarkable degree the fittings of a medieval church. Large clear perpendicular windows admit much light to illuminate the striking colours of the screen, pulpit and altar.

A short walk up a nearby public footpath to **Tornewton** takes one along a delightful valley through limestone country. One of the features of South Devon are these pockets of limestone, and in caves concealed by scrub on either side have been found animal remains from millions of years ago.

Opposite: The Dawlish Water, known locally as the Brook, running through Dawlish

• DAWLISH •

Approaching South Devon down the Exe Estuary, Dawlish (not to be confused with Dawlish Warren) is the first of the south coast holiday resorts to be reached.

The heart of the town is built on both sides of a pleasant open space called the Lawn through which runs the Dawlish Water, or simply the Brook, much frequented by ducks and black swans, who paddle about above some seemingly unconcerned trout. The railway cuts off the view to the sea and creates its own attractions, overpowering the coastal end of the town.

The town is well worth exploring; here and there one can feel the atmosphere that Jane Austen and Charles Dickens must have encountered when they visited Dawlish. (Dickens contrived to have Nicholas Nickleby 'born'

here.) A visit to **Dawlish Museum**, sited in the superb setting of a three-storey Georgian house, will strengthen this feeling.

Dawlish Museum

Barton Terrace, Dawlish. Local history, Victorian room settings, toys, natural history and old photographs. ☎ 01626 865974. Open: May to September, Mondays to Saturdays 10.30am–5pm, Sundays 2–5pm.

• TEIGNMOUTH AND SHALDON •

Teignmouth was largely destroyed by the French in 1690, and was in the frontline, too, in World War II when 79 people were killed in German air raids. Keats stayed at No 20 Northumberland Place with his mother in 1818 — a plaque marks his sojourn.

Above & below: The front at Teignmouth

Teignmouth's buildings reflect its ambivalent outlook. Some splendid nineteenth-century houses look across the seafront open space known as the Den, but at the back of the town are the old, narrower, winding streets. There are two parish churches, and that belonging to West Teignmouth, rebuilt about 1820, has cast-iron pillars airily supporting a roof lantern of unusual delicacy.

Much of Teignmouth's holiday activity takes place near the Den. The pier, theatre, cinema, model railway, tennis and novelty golf are all here. On Dawlish Road is a heated swimming pool. The **museum** is in French Street, so-called as it was built with money given in a public appeal after the 1690 raid.

Teignmouth Museum

29 French Street, Teignmouth. Local history, collection of artefacts from the Armada period vessel wrecked off Church Rocks, railway memorabilia, lace making and prints.
☎ 01626 777041.
Open: Easter, daily 10am–4.30pm. May to September, Monday to Saturday 10am–4.30pm and Sunday 2–4.30pm.

Across the estuary from Teignmouth is Shaldon, reached by a long road bridge (only freed from tolls in 1948); its old toll house stands at the north end, and Shaldon's late nineteenth-century church (completed 1902) is at the south end. This building has been likened to a tunnel of stone, which connoisseurs of Victorian architecture hold in high regard.

The village of **Shaldon**, however, has an air of unspoilt period charm. Lines of simple flower-decked terraced cottages look out on the constantly changing scene of the estuary mouth, at the ferry boats with their lines of imitation gun ports, and perhaps a ball clay ship stuck on one of the ever-shifting sand banks.

At the sea end of the village the great tree-topped headland known as the Ness rears up, and here are found the holiday trappings of the village and the **Shaldon Wildlife Trust**, with a large car park. A tunnel through the cliff to the popular Ness beach is often attributed to smugglers, but they would hardly have advertised their trade in this way; more likely, it was cut during the Napoleonic Wars. On the higher slopes of Shaldon is an approach golf course, and just below the Torquay road is a public park.

2 Torbay to Salcombe

As the county's prime holiday area, South Devon owes its success to three factors: the discovery of its beauty and mild climate at the end of the eighteenth century, when the continent was closed to visitors; the grafting onto these natural characteristics of the social facilities of early watering places such as assembly rooms, accommodation and bathing machines; and the arrival of the Great Western Railway in the late 1840s.

The larger resorts, Torquay and Paignton (now, with Brixham, gathered together under the umbrella title Torbay), are still tossing about in the backwash of the developmental surge which came in the second half of the last century. However in this book, the individuality of the three constituent towns will be retained using the term Tor Bay in its two-word form to describe the natural feature only.

• TORQUAY •

Torquay has an abundance of interest. It began to find favour as a haven for invalids during the time of the Napoleonic Wars, a reputation perpetuated in the present-day Borough motto *Salus et felicitas* – Health and Happiness. At the same time, of course, when the Continent was out of bounds, a few shrewd entrepreneurs, who owned land or added to their estates, built Mediterranean-type villas with Italian-sounding names like Villa Borghese and Villa Como, and were then in a position to re-sell.

Two such families were the Carys and the Palks, and one is not in Torquay long before these names appear in one form or another. Much of Torquay is therefore nineteenth century, though the tall apartment blocks and hotels, some with gull-wing flyaway roofs, are clearly post-World War II.

An exception is the interesting complex of buildings centred on **Torre Abbey**. Here there flourished, from 1196 until the dissolution of the monasteries, an abbey for Premonstratensian canons. It was eventually bought by the Carys in 1665, and it was they who built the present mansion early in the eighteenth century.

The gatehouse probably dates from 1320, and the so-called **'Spanish barn'**, the monastic tithe barn, is another relic from pre-dissolution days. It acquired its name after being used as a temporary prison for 397 Spanish captives from the Armada ship *Nuestra Senora del Rosario* in 1588.

There is one other reminder of olden times within the bounds of Torquay which must be seen – **Cockington.** In the public mind it consists of an ancient forge and Cockington Court, a pleasant but not outstanding mansion in 287

Torre Abbey

Kings Drive, Torquay. Houses Torquay's art collections, works by William Blake, monastic exhibition, a great antiques hunt and Agatha Christie Memorial Room. Extensive gardens and tearoom.
☎ 01803 293593.
Open: Easter to 1st November, daily, 9.30am–6pm.

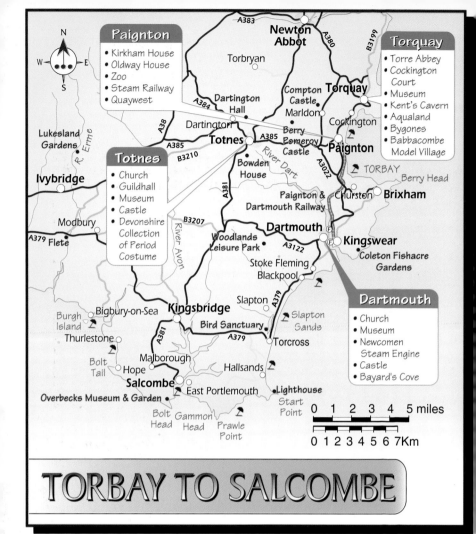

TORBAY TO SALCOMBE

acres (115 hectares) of beautiful grounds. Around this core there are other attractive buildings, notably the Drum Inn (1934) designed by Sir Edwin Lutyens.

Cockington

Torquay. Country park and village, woodland trails, craft centre, working bakery, visitor centre, gardens, restaurants, gift shops. ☎ 01803 607230. Open all year.

The survival of Cockington within Torquay is a considerable achievement, even if a price in tourist exploitation has been paid. Horse-drawn carriages are on hand to take visitors to and from this village within a town.

Sporting possibilities abound with several golf courses, pitch and putt, squash, ten-pin bowling and swimming all there to be tried. Water sports are as varied. Water skiing, windsurfing, sea fishing, sailing or simply taking a boat trip across the bay or round the coast are some of the opportunities available. There are also two cinemas, three theatres, night clubs, discos and casinos.

Torquay offers many other family amusements of all kinds including several museums.

Kent's Cavern

Ilsham Road, Torquay. Man's earliest home in the area — 20,000 to 30,000 years BC.
Caves, sound and light show, exhibitions, guided tours. ☎ 01803 215136. Open: April to September, daily 10am–last tour 4.30pm (but open 9.30am–last tour 5.30pm in July and August). October to March, daily 9am–last tour 4pm. *The Ghosts of Caverns Past* evening tours, late May to early September. ☎ for details of times and dates.

Torquay Museum

529 Babbacombe Road, Torquay. Displays of Devon folk life, pottery, archaeology, Victoriana and many finds from Kent's Cavern. ☎ 01803 293975. Open: April to October, Monday to Saturday 10am–4.45pm; Sunday 1.30–4.45pm. November to March, Monday to Friday 10am–4.45pm.

Brixham Harbour

Babbacombe Model Village is far more than its name implies. It is an internationally-known triumph of landscape miniaturisation, many of the models having sound and animation.

Model Village

Babbacombe, Torquay. Over 400 models, miniature railway, gardens, constantly updated displays. Wheelchair available. ☎ 08103 315315. Open: All year, daily. Easter to June 9.30am–10pm. July/August 9.00am–10pm. September 9.30am–10pm. October 9.30am–9pm. November to Easter 9am–dusk.

On the northern outskirts of the town is **Bygones,** a museum featuring a life-size Victorian street where one can wander back in time.

Bygones

Fore Street, St Marychurch. World War I trench, railway exhibits and model railway. Tearooms and gift shop. ☎ 01803 326108. Open: June to August, Sunday to Thursday, 10am–10pm; Friday and Saturday 10am–6pm. March, April, May, September and October, daily, 10am–6pm. November to February 10am–4pm (5pm weekends and holidays).

Many people enjoy walking along the promenade and the piers. The public gardens entice visitors and a steep climb through the beautiful **Rock End Gardens** behind and above the Imperial Hotel leads to that curiously-named viewpoint, Daddyhole Plain. (A 'daddy' is thought to be a demon in folklore.) The visitor should also walk or motor along the Ilsham Marine Drive, diverting onto the cliffs to get a close look at Thatcher Rock. This is one of the limestone 'horns' of Tor Bay. Berry Head is the other.

• PAIGNTON •

Historically, Paignton was some distance inland — the old streets are unmistakable — but when the railway arrived, the settlement grew towards the station, and soon the rapidly expanding town was filling in the land between the railway and the sea. Fortunately, a pleasant open space was allowed to remain between the front row of buildings and the beach.

Architecturally Paignton is not as distinguished as Torquay, although there are two surprises. **Kirkham House** in Kirkham Street may have been a four-teenth-century priest's house; the public are occasionally allowed to visit its suite of interesting but unfurnished rooms (☎ 01803 522775 for access).

The other surprise, even more unexpected, is an opulent mansion, **Oldway**, built in 1874 for the Singer family (of sewing machine fame) and modelled on Versailles. Now owned by the Council and used largely as offices, it is open to the public as are the equally splendid grounds.

Facing Oldway's main entrance is a round building with a pointed roof, looking rather like a miniature Royal Albert Hall. This was originally built as a riding and exercising pavilion, and may well have been based on the Albert Hall which was built 3 years before Oldway, in 1871.

Paignton Zoo Environmental Park

Totnes Road, Paignton. 75 acres of wood and parkland giving home to many endangered species from around the world. Disabled access. Restaurant, shop. ☎ 01803 527936. Open: All year except Christmas Day 10am–6pm (dusk in winter).

Oldway Mansion

Torquay Road, Paignton. Rows of neo-classical pillars around the exterior prepare one for a sumptuous interior of marble staircases and painted ceilings. ☎ 01803 201201. Open: All year, Monday to Friday 9am–5pm.

Paignton Zoo, the largest in Devon, is a constant delight for visitors. A feature of the zoo are the exotic birds which walk and fly around the grounds. On a tree-covered island in the lake, the gibbons whoop their eerie cries and swing from branch to branch, bringing up their young in cosy barrels loftily sited in the trees.

Before leaving Paignton to explore the countryside nearby, there is a final attraction, the **Paignton and Dartmouth Steam Railway** which uses steam engines to haul trains from the GWR station at Paignton to Kingswear.

Paignton and Dartmouth Steam Railway

Paignton. Special events throughout the year including Santa Specials in December. ☎ 01803 555872. Open: Easter to October, daily.

The railway calls first at Goodrington Sands, then Churston before diving into Greenway tunnel. Emerging, the railway follows the River Dart to Kingswear. A ferry links Kingswear with Dartmouth across the water. At Goodrington Sands, **Quaywest** claims to be Britain's biggest waterpark and includes an awesome waterslide and the highest (and fastest) flume in the country.

Quaywest

Goodrington Sands. Amusements, pools, go-karts, funfair, refreshments. ☎ 01803 555550. Open: Waterpark, Late May to early September, 10am–6pm, 7pm in July and August. Other attractions Easter to end of October, 10am–10pm.

'Behind' Paignton, as it were, are two ancient and historic buildings of the highest interest.

Compton Castle

Marlon, near Torquay. Magical fortified manor house with great hall, spiral staircase and minstrels' gallery. Limited wheelchair access. ☎ 01803 872112. Open: April to October, Monday, Wednesday, Thursday 10am–12.15 and 2–5pm.

Compton Castle nestles in a valley in a seemingly indefensible site about a mile (1.5km) north of the Torbay ring road at Marlon. The earliest part of the building, dating back to about 1330, is the great hall, with later additions of 1450-75 and 1520. Civil War activity is unknown, but by 1750 the hall was ruinous.

The Gilberts – who had included Sir Humphrey Gilbert (founder of Newfoundland) and his half-brother Sir Walter Raleigh – sold Compton Castle in 1800 and bought it back in 1930 before giving it to the National Trust in 1951.

The other historic building is **Berry Pomeroy Castle**, best approached by taking the Totnes road at Marldon Five Lanes and looking for the sign after a few miles.

This is another site where several structures have followed one another, but unlike Compton Castle, the present-day result is a ruin, even if a highly atmospheric one. Three sides could be easily defended; only the south side needed massive walls, and here are the gatehouse, curtain wall and St Margaret's Tower, probably built in the fourteenth century by the Pomeroy family. Between 1548 and 1613 a large mansion was built inside the castle walls by the Seymours; the gaping windows of this abandoned house still taunt us with their mystery. Why was it left to fall down? No-one knows. A fire may be the answer.

Berry Pomeroy Castle

Totnes. Slightly spooky ruined mansion within the remains of a medieval castle and woodland walks.
Open: Easter to October, daily 10am–6pm.

The third of the Tor Bay towns is Brixham, until not so long ago a quiet fishing backwater, but now caught up in the holiday business, though separated from Paignton's southern satellites of Goodrington and Galmpton by a green belt.

Left: The ruined Berry Pomeroy Castle, a quiet location just off the Totnes to Paignton road
Right: The pier at Paignton

• BRIXHAM •

Like Torquay, Brixham sits on limestone. Traces of early man have been found here. In medieval times, the town developed as Higher and Lower Brixham, with the fishing industry concentrated round the creek, which is now largely filled in. The fishing industry was so successful that the ships sought to exploit the fishing grounds of the North Sea, following the migratory shoals, and they were largely responsible for the development of Lowestoft, Grimsby and Fleetwood as fishing ports.

Another nautical connection is the National Coastguard Museum which is incorporated in the **Brixham Museum**. This includes fascinating photographs of wrecks and rescues, and of the kind of apparatus used in saving life around the coast.

Brixham Museum

Bolton Cross, Brixham. Tells the story of Brixham. Displays records relating to the coastguard service.
☎ 01803 856257.
Open: Easter to October, Monday to Friday 10am–5pm, Saturday 10am–1pm.

The harbour at Brixham buzzes with industry most of the time. An extensive inshore fishery survives, and there is much coming and going of holidaymakers' pleasure craft, as well as trips to Torquay or round the coast to Dartmouth.

A worthwhile exploration of **Berry Head Country Park** can well take a couple of hours; there is so much here to see, whether one is interested in plants, sea birds, history or technology. Out to sea are the tankers and supertankers performing their loading or lightening logistics before heading off, shallower in draft, to cope with the Dover Strait, or waiting until the world oil price increases.

The vertical cliffs — do watch children and dogs — provide superb nesting sites for kittiwakes, fulmars, guillemots, gulls of various kinds, kestrels, jackdaws and rock doves; a visit here in the spring is the best time to see hectic avian activity. The limestone rocks carry an unusual flora which includes autumn squill, fellwort, scabious, rock sea lavender and wall pennywort. As several rarities are known here, visitors are asked not to pick specimens.

Across this elevated promontory in Iron Age times the local tribe built a defensive earthwork. The huge Napoleonic War fort, now such a landmark and an interesting feature to explore, destroyed most of this. A certain irony must have been felt by the garrison of that fort when *HMS Bellerophon* put in to Tor Bay bearing Bonaparte to St Helena.

The coastguard station monitors maritime comings and goings, and nearby is Berry Head Lighthouse, which is sometimes said to be the highest, the smallest, and the lowest lighthouse in Great Britain. At 191ft (67m) above sea level there is none higher; being only a few feet high it is very small. Sometimes on a very clear day Portland is visible 35 miles (56km) away across Lyme Bay.

From Berry Head the **South Devon Coast Path** perambulates St Mary's Bay and Sharkham Point, then runs along National Trust land nearly all the way to Kingswear. Much of this magnificent coast was bought by the Trust in late 1982, and is open for public access. At Inner Froward Point is a World War II gun battery, almost complete except for the guns, and inland a little way, on a high point is the 80ft hollow tapering stone pillar known as the Day Mark, an unlit navigational beacon dating back to the 1860s.

• DARTMOUTH •

Two ways of arriving at Kingswear have already been mentioned, by steam train or on foot. Dartmouth, the little town across the water, so redolent of our British heritage, must be in the top ten of any Devonian's list of towns. The charm of the place is its cramped site. Lacking space on the hillsides, Dartmothians have pushed outwards into the river in the same way as their neighbours in Brixham.

In about 1600 the muddy creek of Mill Pool was filled in, to become the lowest part of the present town. The **Market Square** occupies part of this made-up land. Likewise, every building in front of Fairfax Place and Lower Street is built on land reclaimed from the river. Knowing this, it is easier to understand the pressures for space which must have exercised the local merchants. They needed flat land near their ships; there was little point in building high up on the hillsides.

Dartmouth was the leading trading port of Devon. It possessed a deep-water, sheltered anchorage, easily and well-defended by the twin castles of Kingswear and Dartmouth, between which a chain could be strung in times of war.

Dartmouth Castle

Dartmouth. Site of departure of Second and Third Crusades. Church with memorial brasses. Trails in the grounds and picnic areas. ☎ 01803 833588. Open: April to October, daily, 10am–6pm. November to March, Wednesday to Sunday 10am–4pm. Closed 24–26 December and 1 January.

Dartmouth, of course, synonymous with the training of naval officers, is so much a part of our naval tradition that one is almost surprised that the **Royal Naval College** was only built in 1905. Before this, the trainee officers lived in superannuated wooden hulks moored in the Dart, but as these began to rot a permanent building became necessary. The college is officially called Britannia after the first of the hulks it succeeded.

Bayard's Cove, just downstream from the Lower Ferry, is a reminder of these rollicking days of sail. Old buildings line the quay in harmonious disarray.

Other attractive buildings are the seventeenth-century **Butterwalk**, a Grade I listed building containing the comprehensive **Dartmouth Museum**, and St Saviour's Church, with its splendid gallery dating from 1633.

Dartmouth Museum

The Butterwalk, Dartmouth. ☎ 01803 832923. Open: April to October, Mondays to Saturdays 11am–5pm.

Much of the coast south-westwards for 12 miles (2km) belongs to the National Trust, and this includes the wooded hill behind Dartmouth Castle called **Gallants Bower**. On its 400ft (140m) summit is a Civil War earthwork, a relic of the Royalists' determination to hold on to Dartmouth in 1645. However, when the Parliamentarians invested the town, the Royalists put up little resistance, and it soon fell to General Fairfax in January 1646.

The smoke from the steam railway across the Dart prompts one to recall that Thomas Newcomen was born in Dartmouth. Newcomen first recognised the power of steam, and he produced the first industrial steam engine, although James Watt gained most of the credit when he improved the invention 50 years later.

Newcomen Engine House

Mayors Avenue, Dartmouth. A steam engine based on Newcomen's principle, but built in the early nineteenth century. ☎ 01803 834224. Open: January to Easter, November and December, Monday to Saturday 10am–4pm. Easter to October Monday to Saturday 9am–5pm, Sunday 10am–4pm.

Dartmouth's position makes it a good place for boat trips. Pleasure cruises come here from Tor Bay in the summer, and leave Dartmouth for holiday trips along the coast. One of the classic English river journeys is up the Dart to Totnes, a winding, ever-changing voyage of delight. Birdwatchers especially will see much to enchant them.

Above: The South West coast Path is one of the longest routes in Britain and includes both coasts of Devon
Below: Kingswear, across the River Dart from Dartmouth

• TOTNES AND DISTRICT •

Totnes is another of Devon's top ten towns. In 1965 it was recognised by the Council for British Archaeology as of such quality that it was listed as one of the CBA's forty towns 'so splendid and so precious that the ultimate responsibility for them should be regarded as a national concern'.

An exploration of Totnes is best begun from the top end by visiting the **Norman Castle**. As it dominates the town the visitor can quickly get a baron's eye view of Totnes from its walls. The line of the town walls can be picked out, and are traceable on the ground in several places.

Totnes Castle

Totnes. Small but perfect keep stands on its motte beside the inner bailey.
☎ 01803 864406. Open: Easter or 1 April to 30 September, daily 10am–6pm. October, daily 10am–5pm. November to Easter, Wednesday to Sunday 10am–4pm (closed 1–2pm).

Totnes Guildhall

Ramparts Walk, High Street. The council chamber, court room and mayor's parlour contain a great deal of interest.
☎ 01803 862147. Open: April to October, Monday to Friday, 10am–1pm and 2–5pm.

Down **High Street** are the two covered pavement arcades of the **Butterwalk** and the **Poultry Walk**, similar to other pillared ambulatories at Dartmouth, Kingsbridge and Plympton. The red sandstone church is worth a visit. The Beer stone rood screen is notable as a superb example of fifteenth-century stone carving. At the 'back' of the churchyard is the **Guildhall**, built in 1533. The Ramparts Walk leads to the East Gate, where High Street gives way to Fore Street.

After passing through **East Gate, Totnes Museum** is on the right An unusual exhibit relates to early computers. Charles Babbage the 'father' of British computer science spent much of his early life in Totnes; he virtually invented the punch-card system and a kind of prototype computer, the analytical engine. He was far ahead of his time and like many such men of genius was not appreciated or understood in his lifetime.

Alongside the River Dart at Totnes with the castle in the background

Totnes Museum

Totnes. Excellent local history museum in a half-timbered building. ☎ 01803 863821. Open: April to October, Monday to Friday 10.30am–5pm, Bank Holidays 11am–3pm.

Devonshire Collection of Period Costume

Bogan House, 43 High Street, Totnes. ☎ 01803 862423. Open: Late May to end of September, Monday to Friday 11am–5pm.

The house occupied by the museum is only one of many which preserve their original form, but may have false or later façades, belying their age. A notable feature of many of these early town houses is their decorated plaster ceilings.

Across the road, set in the pavement, is the **Brutus Stone**. A legend links this lump of rock with the Trojan who landed here in 1000 BC. Opposite is Atherton Lane, often festively floral.

The main street is so crammed with historic buildings that it is worthwhile to walk up and down on opposite pavements. Opposite the Civic Hall is the **Devonshire Collection of Period Costume** in 43 High Street. It is well worth a visit to see beautiful things delightfully displayed. Indeed, Totnes on summer Tuesdays has local people, mostly shopkeepers, dressed in Elizabethan costume.

At the top of the town, not far from the large car park, are the **Leech Wells** in Leechwell Lane. Water gushes into three stone troughs, and the lepers came here in an attempt to cleanse themselves in what they thought were healing waters.

One mile south of Totnes off the A381 is **Bowden House**, a Tudor dwelling with a Queen Anne façade.

Bowden House

Totnes. Incorporates the British Photographic Museum. House reputedly haunted. Guides in Georgian costume. Café and shop. ☎ 01803 863664. Open: April to October, Monday to Thursday from 12 noon.

Also to the south, near Blackawton, is the **Woodlands Leisure Park** with a huge number of rides and slides (wet and dry) and several play areas.

Woodlands Leisure Park

A3122, 5 miles west of Dartmouth. Activities and entertainment for all the family. Animals and birds, falconry centre, nature trail.
Refreshments and shop. Wheelchair access.
☎ 01803 712598.
Open: mid-March to mid-November daily from 9.30am.

Continuing up the Dart Valley, the next stop is at **Shinner's Bridge**, where the A384 and A385 meet, our first encounter with 'Dartington'. This many-sided concept began in 1925, when Leonard and Dorothy Elmhirst, both idealists, purchased an 820-acre (328 hectares) run-down estate centred on **Dartington Hall**, with the intention of reviving life in the countryside.

Since then, the activities at Dartington have blossomed and multiplied. Activities over the years have included building, forestry, a visitor centre, education (adult courses and a boarding school) and the arts in the broadest sense.

Cider Press Centre

Shinners Bridge, Dartington. Visitor and craft centre for Dartington Hall where one can buy furniture, good quality gifts, farm foods, clothes and tweed cloth, and eat (except on Sundays) at an excellent vegetarian restaurant, Cranks. ☎ 01803 864171. Open: All year, Monday to Saturday 9.30am–5.30pm. Also open on Sunday, 10.30am–5.30pm from Easter to Christmas.

Various walks around the estate begin from the Cider Press car park, some short, some long. Dartington Hall itself ought to be visited; but, as it is about 1 mile (1.5km) from Shinner's Bridge, one can turn off the A384 at Dartington church and park in the hall car park. The courtyard is under the arch, and opposite is the Great Hall, a roofless ruin in 1925, but now beautifully restored with timbers drawn from the estate. A chamber music concert here is a sublime experience.

Behind the hall in the gardens is the restored tilting yard, with terraced grassy banks and twelve enormous clipped yews looking like giant skittles. Modern tournaments, outdoor plays, masques and son et lumière presentations are held here.

• FROM DARTINGTON TO KINGSBRIDGE •

The rest of this chapter deals with that part of Devon known as the South Hams. There is no general agreement about exact boundaries, but the Rivers Yealm (pronounced 'Yam') and Dart on the west and east, Dartmoor to the north and the sea to the south, are usually reckoned to define this fertile rural area of farms and villages.

Start Point lighthouse

After several switchback miles, the road drops down to sea level at the north end of **Slapton Sands**, a $2^{1}/_{2}$ mile (4km) bank of shingle and pebbles, thrown up when the glaciers melted after the last Ice Age. Trapped behind this pebble ridge are the waters of Slapton Ley, the largest natural freshwater lake in Devon, and divided into the Higher and Lower Ley by the road leading to the village of Slapton.

The remains of Hallsands near to Start Point

The A379 coast road from Dartmouth dips, climbs and winds through the villages of Stoke Fleming and Strete, and past **Blackpool Sands**, an attractive cove overhung with Monterey pines, and bearing no resemblance to its north country namesake. The local people repulsed a Breton invasion force here in 1404.

World War II Memorial

At Slapton Sands, the tall stone memorial obelisk by the roadside — unveiled by the United States General Grunther in 1954 — commemorates the use of the area in late 1943 and early 1944 for beach landing practice prior to the Normandy invasion.

The **Higher Ley**, being smaller and shallower, and receiving the largest stream, the River Gara, has silted up in the thousands of years since it was created, and is now largely reed-grown and bordered with willow.

The Lower Ley, however, is open water, fringed with reed. The eels, roach and perch fall prey to the pike, as do frogs and ducklings. As a pike fishery the Ley is highly thought of; but it is as a bird sanctuary that the Ley is so important. The scarcity of other freshwater ponds and lakes in the south-west makes Slapton Ley a place of avian concentration, particularly in the spring, and when birds are migrating in the autumn.

This diversity of natural interest was the origin of the Slapton Ley Field Centre, set up between the sea and the village. The Field Studies Council runs courses here for many categories of study and student. Two nature trails have been laid down round the Lower Ley, and leaflets describing the routes are available from the Centre. Guided walks are advertised in the summer.

The village of **Slapton** should be visited, too; a pleasing hotchpotch of buildings in the South Hams tradition. The church porch contains a sanctuary ring. In medieval times, it was sufficient to touch it to receive sanctuary, but there then followed a complicated ritual of confession and abjuration which resulted in the felon having to leave the country. Near the church are the ruins of the chantry, of which the tower is all that now remains.

Along the coast road is **Torcross**, an exposed village partly built on the pebble ridge itself. A World War II Sherman tank, recovered from the sea, is on display in the car park as a memorial to some 800 USA servicemen who perished during Operation Tiger in 1944. Torcross is periodically battered by gales, but has not so far suffered the fate of Hallsands 3 miles (5km) to the south, almost at Start Point. To reach Hallsands, turn left off the A379 in Stokenham and follow the road signs.

Since it is so close, one should visit **Start Point Lighthouse**, which dates from 1836. The light has a range of 20.8 miles (33km). The name Start comes from the same Anglo-Saxon root *steort* meaning a tail, which is found in the name of the bird, the redstart.

From Start Point there is a way through the lanes to East Prawle; the route is then signposted to **Prawle Point**, 1 mile (1.5km) further on. This is the southern

Hallsands

Hallsands was a row of 37 houses on a rocky ledge beneath the cliff, protected by a shingle foreshore.

The men earned a living by fishing, and life was uneventful until the closing years of the last century, when a contractor engaged in construction work at Devonport dockyard was given permission to dredge shingle offshore causing the beach level to drop 13ft (4.5m). Its natural defences dissipated, the village was exposed to the sea, and in a series of storms all the houses were demolished, the last in 1917. The whole affair was a case of official buck-passing, and little was done for the homeless.

The line of ruined buildings can be seen beneath the cliff, and it is surprising that houses were built there in the first place.

To continue the exploration of the South Hams, the A379 leads to Kingsbridge, the 'capital' of this part of Devon. All roads lead to **Kingsbridge**, the natural route centre at the head of the Kingsbridge Estuary. This wide expanse of water, with many shallow creeks poking tidal tentacles among fertile fields, is not fed by any large river.

Although the channel to Salcombe is used by pleasure boats and yachts, 80 years ago a weekly 'market packet' steamer ran between Kingsbridge and Plymouth, calling at Salcombe on the way. Ships from far-off places used to tie up to discharge exotic cargoes, and export cider, corn, harness and stone. Ships were built nearby, and the recreation ground is on the site of a tidal millpond.

Between Kingsbridge and the sea are the remains of 22 lime-kilns; the limestone came by sea from Plymouth.

Kingsbridge is now a busy, cheerful place with good shops, pubs and restaurants. The appearance of the town is attractive, though there are few outstanding buildings. Perhaps **The Shambles** is the most striking structure. Here the old market building is raised on Elizabethan granite pillars. In **Fore Street** there are quaint passages and alleys on either side. Kingsbridge passages have curious names like Squeezebelly Passage, Khartoum Place, Baptist Lane and several named after inns.

At the top of the town, on the east side of the road, is **Knowle House**, one of several

extremity of the county. There is a National Trust car park at the road end, a few hundred yards from the Point itself. Start Point is just out of sight beyond Peartree Point, but the other direction looks across the mouth of Salcombe Harbour to Bolt Head.

fine eighteenth- and nineteenth-century houses. This one was the home of Colonel Montagu, who gave his name to the Montagu's harrier.

On the opposite side of the road, and lower down, is the very interesting **Cookworthy Museum** in the Old Grammar School. William Cookworthy (1705-80), the English discoverer of china clay, who made the first English porcelain, was born in Kingsbridge.

Cookworthy Museum

Fore Street, Kingsbridge. Exhibition sponsored by English China Clays Ltd. There are also interesting displays of agriculture and domestic life. ☎ 01548 853235. Open: Late March to end of October, Monday to Saturday 10am–5pm. Last admission 4.30pm.

• SALCOMBE •

Salcombe is a drive of 7 miles (11km) through West Alvington and Malborough. Look for Malborough's church spire, a prominent landmark for miles around. The problem at Salcombe in high summer may be finding a parking space, but it is worth the effort! Everyone in Salcombe in July and August seems to be in the boat business. Blue jeans, guernseys and yellow boat boots are as common as top hats at Ascot for this is a sailing centre. Salcombe is also a retirement base, the salubrious climate of Devon's southernmost town helping to make it so.

Salcombe Museum of Maritime and Local History

Town Hall Basement, Salcombe. Includes details of the Slapton World War II battle training area.
☎ 01548 843927 (Tourist Information Centre).
Open: Easter to October, daily 10.30am–12.30pm, 2.30–4.30pm.

The busy waterfront at Salcombe

Salcombe's fame in history is concerned with her fleet of yacht-like clipper schooners, which always brought home the first fruits from the pineapple pickings in the West Indies or the orange harvest in the Azores. Local trades are well portrayed in the Salcombe **Museum of Maritime and Local History** at Custom House Quay.

Another collection of bygones is at the **Overbecks Museum** at **Overbecks House** (National Trust) at the southern end (Sharpitor) of the built-up area.

Overbecks Museum and Garden

Sharpitor, Salcombe. Edwardian house containing a miscellany of maritime artefacts. Wheelchair access. Tearoom. Shop. ☎ 0154 842893. Open: Museum April to July, daily except Saturday 11am–5.30pm; August, daily 11am–5.30pm; September, Sunday to Friday 11am–5.30pm; October, Sunday to Thursday 11am–5pm. Garden all year, daily 10am–8pm or sunset if earlier.

Overbecks House also accommodates **Salcombe Youth Hostel**, and looks over the dreaded Salcombe Bar, a sea-covered sand spit waiting to snag deep-keeled ships, especially at low tide in a storm. In 1916, thirteen of the crew of fifteen of the Salcombe lifeboat were lost in turbulent seas on Salcombe Bar. This hazard may have inspired Tennyson's famous poem *Crossing the Bar*.

• WESTWARDS FROM SALCOMBE •

Beyond Hope Cove, which nestles behind the protecting arm of Bolt Tail, the coastline changes in character. Tall cliffs give way to a mixture of low cliffs, sand dunes and popular beaches. Inner Hope is a piece of Devon miraculously preserved from a hundred years ago, a square of thatched cottages unspoilt by modern development.

One aspect of the man-made South Hams landscape which remains to be remarked upon is the massive masonry gateposts. Instead of using a wooden post, farmers in times past — the date unknown — built up buttresses of stone on which to hang their gates, and went to some trouble to make a feature of them, though no-one is quite certain why.

Off **Thurlestone** (the name means 'holed stone') is the famous arched rock which gave the parish its name, and after the small estuary of the Avon, **Bigbury-on-Sea** is reached, with its sands, shops and sea tractor. This strange contraption is employed to maintain the link between **Burgh Island** and the mainland when the tide is in. It can operate in 10ft (3.5m) of water and cope with seas up to a force nine gale. A large hotel dominates the island and the Pilchard Inn provides refreshments.

One further popular beach, **Challaborough**, will be found along this stretch of coast before access becomes difficult (unless the continuous South Devon Coast Path is used). The next estuary belongs to the Erme, which at low tide may be waded from slipway to slipway, but care must be taken especially during stormy weather or when there is a good deal of floodwater coming down river.

Looking towards Thurlestone Rock

Plymouth & District

Plymouth Hoe

The city of **Plymouth** has one of the finest natural sites in Britain, and ranks with Edinburgh, Bath, Cambridge and Bristol for position and historic interest. The deep, wide and fast-flowing waters of the River Tamar effectively prevented much westward expansion of Plymouth into Cornwall until the railway bridges were built across the Tamar and Tavy.

Just across the water, at Mount Batten, much evidence was turned up early this century of an Iron Age and Roman settlement, perhaps lasting for a thousand years.

There are other hazy descriptions of Roman and Dark Age settlement, but what is undisputed is the development of medieval Plymouth round Sutton Harbour and the area to the north-west. St Andrew's Church on the present Royal Parade is

an ancient foundation, and Old Town Street nearby has an early origin; so the Plymouth of the Middle Ages should be sought in the arc encompassed by the mouth of Sutton Harbour, behind New Street to St Andrew's Church, north to Old Town Street and back to the waterfront on the east side of Sutton Harbour.

Plymouth however, being nearer the open sea, was more vulnerable to raids, and in 1403

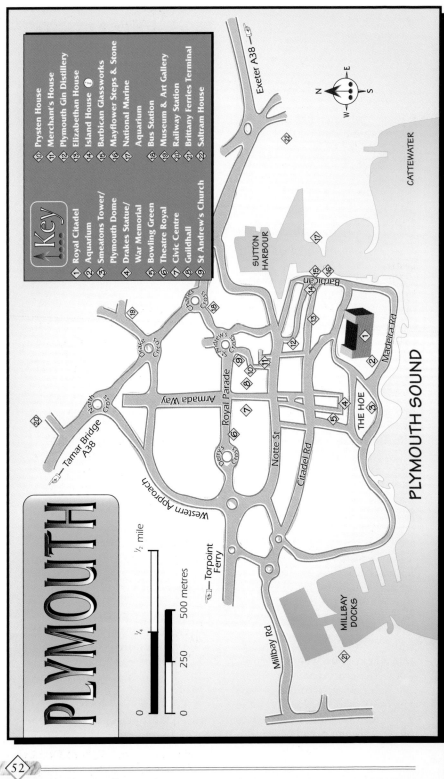

PLYMOUTH

Key

1. Royal Citadel
2. Aquarium
3. Smeatons Tower/
   Plymouth Dome
4. Drakes Statue/
   War Memorial
5. Bowling Green
6. Theatre Royal
7. Civic Centre
8. Guildhall
9. St Andrew's Church
10. Prysten House
11. Merchant's House
12. Plymouth Gin Distillery
13. Elizabethan House
14. Island House ℹ
15. Barbican Glassworks
16. Mayflower Steps & Stone
17. National Marine
    Aquarium
18. Bus Station
19. Museum & Art Gallery
20. Railway Station
21. Brittany Ferries Terminal
22. Saltram House

PLYMOUTH SOUND

CATTEWATER

SUTTON HARBOUR

Barbican

Madeira Rd

THE HOE

Citadel Rd

Notte St

Royal Parade

Armada Way

St Andrew's Cross

Charles Cross

Drake Circus

North Cross

Derry's Cross

Western Approach

Tamar Bridge A38

Exeter A38

Torpoint Ferry

Millbay Rd

MILLBAY DOCKS

0   250   500 metres
0   ¼   ½ mile

a large French force attacked the town and burnt 600 houses. The inhabitants asked for a wall to be built round the town although only the names of the gates remain today, Old Town Gate and Hoe Gate, for instance. One end of the wall was built against Plymouth Castle, and that too has all but disappeared. The name Barbican, now widely applied to the area of New Street and Southside Street, is derived from a part of this castle.

The part of Plymouth known by Drake and his captains, and, later, by the Pilgrim Fathers sailing on the *Mayflower* was, therefore, Sutton. Plymouth sided with Parliament in the Civil War and suffered a 3-year siege. It was King William of Orange, who authorised the building of the dockyard on virgin land fronting the Tamar Estuary, where it is called the Hamoaze.

This immediately pulled development across the intervening land and Stonehouse grew, as it was situated halfway between the growing town of Dock and Plymouth itself. During the Napoleonic Wars the upstart Dock (32,000 people) outstripped its neighbour Plymouth (22,000) and Stonehouse (6,000), and in 1824 was granted the dignity of the name Devonport.

Nearer our own time, in 1914, the so-called 'Three Towns' were amalgamated into one municipal authority to become Plymouth. The city suffered disastrous air raids in World War II, and much of the centre was destroyed. St Andrew's Church and the Guildhall were both gutted, but have been rebuilt.

The walk starts beside the **Civic Centre** where Armada Way intersects Royal Parade.

With your back to the main shopping centre, look along Armada Way where it rises gently up to the Hoe with the Naval War Memorial prominent in the view. About halfway up is the massive anchor which once belonged to the *Ark Royal*, and beside where you are standing is the civic flagstaff, a shaft rising from a replica of Drake's Drum. The unveiling of this memorial in 1947 by the King marked the start of the re-building of the new Plymouth.

On the left is the **Guildhall**, dating from 1873, but gutted in 1941 and rebuilt after the war, somewhat altered.

St Andrew's Church is the largest parish church in Devon, and, as it stands, is a post-war restoration, completed in 1957. It possesses some very striking modern stained glass, which may not be to everyone's taste.

Leaving the church through the south door, the **Prysten House,** the oldest building remaining in Plymouth, is opposite. The priests from Plympton Priory were probably accommodated here while ministering at the church.

Prysten House

Finewell Street. Variety of unusual features. Carved bishop's throne. Model of Plymouth as it looked in 1620. Plymouth tapestry depicting the life and times of the Prysten House. ☎ 01752 661414. Open: April to October, Monday to Saturday, 9am–4pm.

The Merchant's House

Palace Street.
Interesting objects
relating to Plymouth's
past. Victorian pharmacy.
☎ 01752 304774.
Open: Easter to end of
September, Tuesday to
Friday 10–5.30pm,
Saturday 10am–5pm.
Closed 1–2pm.

Leaving the Prysten House, turn right and right again to see the **Merchant's House** in St Andrew's Street. This sixteenth-century four-storey town house is the best example in Plymouth of a well-to-do entrepreneur's dwelling. William Parker, an Elizabethan privateer, merchant and mayor of Plymouth, was living in the house in 1608.

Above: The Merchant's House, Plymouth
Below: The ancient Quay Road, Sutton Harbour, Plymouth

Walk down St Andrew's Street, left into Notte Street and right into Southside Street, where on the right is the Spirit of Plymouth **Blackfriars Distillery** building. This seems to have been a friary long before Coates Gin Co came on the scene in 1793, and the refectory, with a fine arch-braced timber roof, is open to the public.

Blackfriars Distillery

60 Southside Street.
Friary remains and
distillery tours. ☎ 01752
665292. Open: Easter to
end of October, Monday
to Saturday from
10.30am–4.45pm.

Southside Street, with its neat lamps bracketed to the shop fronts, is a pleasant busy street with shops selling secondhand books, antique prints and the better type of gifts, and there are several restaurants and public houses. It once looked directly out on Sutton Harbour.

The north side of the street with its 'opes' (an opening onto a water-front) breaking it up into small blocks, was built later. Through one of them, on the left, one can see the enormous **Barbican Mural** by Plymouth artist Robert Lenkiewicz at the closed end of Quay Road.

Now follow the quay round the western side of Sutton Harbour. The early nineteenth-century Custom House faces the old Custom House of the Tudor period, now given over to other uses. This is a lively part of Plymouth, with much fishing boat activity and the fish market where the public can buy fish too.

Continuing with the theme of underwater life, a short walk across the lock at the entrance to Sutton Harbour is the new **National Marine Aquarium**. Here in a state-of-the-art setting is a breathtaking display of ocean life, from the smallest sea creatures to magnificent sharks.

Returning to the western side of the harbour the **Mayflower Stone** can be seen, marking the departure point of the Pilgrim Fathers in 1620, one of several memorials to great events which have started from this spot.

Across the way from here is **Island House**, a building standing on its own, dating from about

National Marine Aquarium

The Barbican, Plymouth. Expert talks, conservation in action, shark theatre, living coral reef, seawater wave tank. Wheelchair access to all displays. Shop. Café. ☎ 01752 220084. Open: daily (except Christmas Day) 10am–6pm.

1590, where tradition says some of the pilgrims lodged prior to their departure for North America. A board on the outside wall lists those who travelled aboard the *Mayflower*.

Behind Island House is New Street, an attractive narrow cobbled highway, the actual stone road surface of which is 'listed' being of historic importance. The original carved door frames are on Nos 34, 35, 37 and 38, and No 32 is an **Elizabethan house**. This original house of about 1584 was well restored from near dereliction in 1926. Notice the ship's mast round which the spiral staircase wraps itself. A rope steadies anyone using the stairs, another nautical touch. Through No 40 is a pleasant little garden, where plants known to have been cultivated in Tudor times are grown.

The Elizabethan House

Barbican. Tudor sea captain's timber framed dwelling. Period furniture and furnishings. ☎ 01752 253871. Open: April to October, Wednesday to Sunday 10am–5pm.

At the foot of New Street, Madeira Road has the last remaining ruin of old Plymouth Castle on the right, beneath the massive walls of the **Royal Citadel** (1666), still used as barracks for the Royal Marines. Guided tours take visitors round the walls at certain times. The baroque gateway is considered the finest in Britain.

Royal Citadel

Madeira Road. Guided tours of England's principal 17th-century fortress. ☎ 01752 775841. Open: May to end of September. Tours 2pm and 3.30pm daily.

In the opposite direction, the Cattewater, the actual mouth of the Plym, is where Drake's fleet anchored. Round the corner, **Plymouth Breakwater** comes into view. This immense civil engineering project made Plymouth a much safer port, especially in the days of sail, though paradoxically, when it was completed in 1847, having been 35 years in the making, powered ships were beginning to be built. It is almost a mile long and contains 3,620,440 tons of local limestone.

Tucked in a sea-facing site on the slopes of the Hoe is **Plymouth Dome** where the whole story of Plymouth is told under one roof, with the panorama of Plymouth Sound just outside the windows. An even better view can be enjoyed from the top of **Smeaton's Tower**, the Eddystone Lighthouse of 1759, moved to its present site in 1884, having been superseded in 1882 by Douglass's present lighthouse. On a clear day the tower can be seen on its rock 14 miles (22km) out at sea. The cramped quarters will perhaps surprise the visitor.

Plymouth Dome

The Hoe. A high-tech, award-winning interpretation centre for all the family. Elizabethan street. The Great Seafarers and their voyages. Audio visual displays. Disabled access. Gift Shop. Café. Admission includes visit to Smeaton's Tower. ☎ 01752 600608. Open: All year, daily from 9am. Tower open Easter to end of October, 10am–4.30pm.

Until it was destroyed in the Plymouth blitz, the 1884 promenade pier jutted out from the Hoe and provided a venue for concerts and dancing. On the Hoe itself, an elevated promenade gives views one way to the sea, and the other along the $^3/_4$ mile (1km) Armada Way. The Hoe gives the finest view of Plymouth Sound, where countless epic voyages have begun and ended, from the naval task force against the Armada to the more recent one against the Argentinians in the Falklands.

Also on the Hoe is the enormous **Naval War Memorial**, surmounted by a dented globe. The damage was caused by a barrage balloon in World War II. Around its base are the names of 22,443 men who lost their lives in both wars. There are other monuments; the National Armada Memorial, one to the Boer War, while the jaunty figure of Sir Francis Drake looks out to sea, a copy statue of one at Tavistock, his birthplace. Not far away, probably where the Royal Citadel was later built, he is supposed to have been playing bowls when the Armada was spotted.

To return to the starting point on Royal Parade, walk north to Citadel Road. Turn left here, and follow Citadel Road to Millbay Road and the site of the old Millbay Station (opened 1849, closed 1941). In the great days of transatlantic sea travel, ships from the USA would put in to Plymouth Sound, to land those passengers in a hurry to reach London, before resuming their journey up Channel.

Before leaving the city centre it is worth paying a visit to the **Plymouth Museum and Art Gallery**, which occupies one of the few buildings in the city to survive the bombing.

Plymouth Museum & Art Gallery

By Drake Circus. Its collections are strong on Plymouth porcelain, Plymouth silver and paintings by local artists including Sir Joshua Reynolds. Local archaeology and natural history.
☎ 01752 304774.
Open: All year, Tuesday to Friday 10am–5.30pm. Saturday 10am–5pm.

Whilst this walk covers the obvious attractions of Plymouth, further exploration perhaps with the assistance of public transport, will reveal unexpected architectural finds and fine views around the Tamar estuary. Ker Street, Devonport in particular has some interesting buildings relating to past times.

Because so much is owned by HM Government, such places as the Dockyard, Stonehouse Hospital, the King William Yard and the Citadel are not usually open to the public, but the Dockyard, for instance, may be open one day a year for what used to be called Plymouth Navy Day: some ships may be visited.

• THE PLYMOUTH COASTLINE •

The best way to get to know Plymouth's dissected coastline is to take a boat trip from Mayflower Steps as far as possible up the Tamar. The point where the boat turns back will depend on the tide, but if it reaches as far as Weir Head or Morwellham, the trip will take 5 or 6 hours. Other cruises from Phoenix Wharf go outside Plymouth Sound past the Breakwater and the Great Mew Stone to the Yealm Estuary.

Further afield, about 4 miles (6km) east of the centre of Plymouth, is the delightful small town of **Plympton St Maurice**, older than its amorphous municipal neighbour, but now a sleepy backwater. Plympton Grammar School, built in 1664 and restored in 1870, is remarkable for the painters it has produced. England's finest portrait painter, Sir Joshua Reynolds, was educated here.

The town, particularly Fore Street, is unspoilt, with its Guildhall jutting out over the pavement and covered Butterwalk. None of the buildings is in the top bracket, but together they make a very pleasing harmonious group.

Not far away is **Saltram House** (National Trust), the largest house in Devon: other superlatives apply equally. Because of Sir Joshua Reynolds' lifelong association with the owners, the Parkers, it contains many paintings by him and is the only complete example in south-west England of Robert Adams' interior design.

The house was begun in the late sixteenth century, but has been considerably changed over the years, the last alteration being in 1820, when John Foulston added the Doric porch and other exterior refinements.

Inside, the rooms which startle and sparkle with eighteenth-century freshness are the saloon and the dining room. Neither is lit by electricity; both have Axminster carpets reflecting, but not imitating, the delicate design of the ceilings. To stand in these rooms is an unusual experience, for one is literally surrounded by beauty, all so delicately done as not to be overpowering. Reached from outside is the Great Kitchen, with a variety of old utensils on show. The gardens are of the informal kind, with trees and shrubs predominating.

The ring of forts was continued around Plymouth's northern (landward) approaches, and they represent the climax of British castellar architecture. Never again were defences on

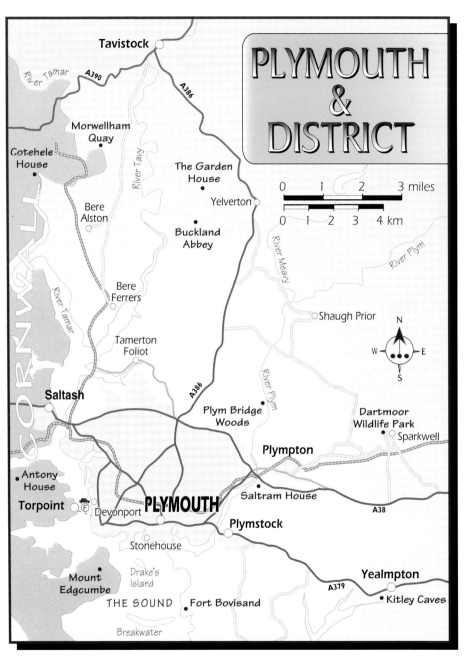

PLYMOUTH & DISTRICT

such a heroic scale constructed in Great Britain. An excellent example of one of these forts, which is open to the public, is **Crownhill Fort** just north of Plymouth city centre.

Saltram House

Plympton. George II mansion with original contents. Restored orangery (1775), chapel (1776) (now an art gallery) and folly-type structures in grounds. Wheelchair access, lift to first floor. Shop and restaurant. ☎ 01752 336546. Open: Easter to end of October, Sunday to Thursday and Good Friday: house and garden 12.30–5.30pm (11.30am opening on Sundays and Bank Holidays, 4.30pm closing in October). Garden also open on Saturdays and Sundays in March 11am–4pm.

Crownhill Fort

Off Tavistock Road, Plymouth. Largest and least altered of the Victorian forts. Nineteenth-century canons, barrack rooms, parade ground. Regular events depicting Victorian military life. ☎ 01752 793754. Open: End of March to end of October, daily 10am–5pm.

On the north-eastern outskirts of Plymouth and getting up into the foothills of Dartmoor the visitor will find the **Dartmoor Wildlife Park** at Sparkwell. Really a zoo, the illusion of animals in their natural setting is obtained by allowing them space and encouraging trees to grow, with a minimum of wire fencing and iron bars, though (obviously) the tigers and wolves are securely enclosed! Visitors are allowed to mix with the more friendly birds and animals.

Just out of Plymouth, up the Plym Valley, are **Plym Bridge Woods** (National Trust). A remarkable survival of woodland, only $3\frac{1}{2}$ miles (5.5km) from the centre of Plymouth, this strip of beautiful varied country is not quite 2 miles (3.2km) long, by half a mile wide, but it contains a truly incredible collection of industrial archaeological interest: the tracks of three old railways and the Cann quarry canal.

Deer are often seen in the woods, and adders favour the habitat provided by the discarded slabs of slate in the enormous spoil heaps. Devon County Council has negotiated a continuous recreational footpath up the Plym Valley beyond Plym Bridge Woods to link up with the Dartmoor National Park at Shaugh Bridge.

Dartmoor Wildlife Park

Sparkwell, near Plymouth. Hands-on experience of animals where possible, falconry centre, comprehensive Big Cat collection. Daily events. Shop, restaurant, and picnic area. ☎ 01752 837209. Open: All year, daily 10am–6pm.

• THE TAMAR AND THE TAVY •

Once across the north-striking A386 the land dips to the valleys of the Tavy and Tamar, the former a private and wooded river, the latter more open, larger, and carrying on its tidal waters considerable recreational traffic. A hundred years ago much commercial transport also used the Tamar.

Saltram House

The undulating peninsula between the two rivers is occupied by the small town of **Bere Alston** on the top and the ancient parish centre of **Bere Ferrers** by the estuary edge of the Tavy. The area is still served by a branch railway line from Plymouth, which crosses both rivers by large viaducts and stops at Bere Ferrers and Bere Alston, before terminating in Cornwall at Gunnislake. The line is a delight to use.

Communications were always difficult in this hilly landscape, and the rivers were used extensively until the railways arrived. The old quays are peaceful now and pleasant places to while away an hour or two. On the south and

The former pub at Morwellham Quay

west facing slopes, vast quantities of strawberries are grown. Bere Ferrers church is one of the most interesting in Devon, with much fourteenth-century work, and a canopied tomb to Sir William de Ferrers and his wife.

Overlooking the Tavy Valley near Yelverton is Sir Francis Drake's old home, **Buckland Abbey** (National Trust), like the rest of this corner of Devon, a peaceful retreat. Amicia, Countess of Devon, founded the abbey in 1278, and white-robed Cistercian brothers came to Buckland from the Isle of Wight to establish their estate.

At the dissolution the property was initially leased to George Pollard, but in 1541 the king sold the abbey to Sir Richard Grenville. His son, Roger, was the commander of the *Mary Rose* which sank with all hands in the Solent in 1545. The hulk of the ship has now been raised and put on show in Portsmouth. The next two tenants of Buckland Abbey were also to die at sea, notably Sir Richard Grenville (the son of Roger) of the *Revenge*. The buildings in the meantime had been converted into a country house, though their monastic ancestry is obvious.

At this point Francis Drake comes on the scene. Born not far away, outside Tavistock, he was looking for a property not far from Plymouth, which would match his new-found fame. In 1581 he purchased the estate from his rival Grenville, via two intermediaries and, as Sir Francis, he moved in, then aged 36. He had already achieved the circumnavigation of the world, but his victory over the Spanish Armada was still 7 years away. He died of dysentery on the Spanish Main in 1596, childless. Fortunately his brother Thomas was with him when he died and must have brought home Francis' drum, **Drake's Drum**, such a treasure from those stirring days, and it is still on view at Buckland Abbey.

Buckland Abbey

Yelverton. Sir Francis Drake memorabilia, history exhibitions, monastic barn, craft workshops, herb garden and delightful walks. Wheelchair access. Restaurant and shop. ☎ 01822 853607. Open: April to October, daily except Thursday 10.30am–5.30pm. November to March, Saturday and Sunday 2–5pm. Last admission 45mins before closing.

Life went on, with the Drake heirs, through Thomas, occupying the abbey. A skirmish occurred there during the Civil War in 1643, and a serious fire which broke out in 1938 was put out before it did irreparable damage. In 1942 Captain Meyrick, the last Drake to live there, sold the property to Captain Rodd, who gave the estate to the National Trust; after repairs it was opened to the public by Lord Mountbatten in 1951. Considerable restoration work has recently been undertaken.

• TAVISTOCK •

Keeping to the valley of the Tavy, the next place of substance is Tavistock, the most attractive, after Totnes, of Devon's inland towns, its character wrought by the mixture of a good natural site, the presence of certain minerals in commercial quantities, a good building stone, and enterprising landowners.

Tavistock made little impression on history until a Benedictine abbey was established near a Saxon *stoc* (a stockade or enclosure) about 974, and this part of the present-day name is the lasting memorial to the early settlement.

The abbey became enormously wealthy, and a neighbouring borough developed, with its own market and fair. When the monasteries were dissolved in 1539, the town and much land nearby were bought by the Russell family, from whom sprang the Dukes of Bedford.

With the discovery of workable quantities of tin on Dartmoor in the twelfth century, Tavistock became one of the three stannary towns on the edge of Dartmoor. (The other two were Ashburton and Chagford.) Tin, however, made but a small impact compared with what was to come later.

The Dartmoor tin was worked out in the early years of the seventeenth century, and Tavistock turned briefly to producing cloth; but this in turn failed. However, copper was fortunately discovered nearby at Mary Tavy in large quantities in the 1790s, and this caused a kind of West Devon copper 'rush'.

The Russells, curiously, were no more anxious to exploit this underground wealth than the abbots had been to develop tin; but eventually they submitted to local pressure, and the appearance of Tavistock today is largely derived from the rebuilding they carried out. Tavistock is virtually a nineteenth-century new town.

At first sight, the abbey ruins are disappointingly incomplete, built over and around by later construction. But there are several significant parts visible within 150 yards (136.5m) of Bedford Square. Betsy Grimball's Tower beside the Bedford Hotel, and the Still Tower and abbey wall on the river bank, are the most substantial and unaltered remains. Who Betsy Grimball was, nobody knows.

Next to the Post Office is a dining hall, preserved intact though with one end altered, and now a nonconformist place of worship, and the large Gothic gate across the way was the main entrance to the abbey.

The parish church stood on its present site when the abbey was a going concern and served the common people of the neighbourhood. There is an especially good monument to Sir John Glanvill in the Lady Chapel, and the modern William Morris glass in the north-east window is worth a detailed study.

Bedford Square is a product of the Victorian age, an expression of civic pride shared by the Duke of Bedford and the citizens. This duke, Francis, now looks straight down his boulevard, Plymouth Road, from his plinthed statue at another more famous Francis, Drake, who stands at the western entrance to the town. Francis Drake is believed to have been born at Crowndale, just outside Tavistock, but while there are no other claimants, proof is lacking.

Beside the Drake statue is the rebuilt gatehouse of the Fitzford estate. Hard by the gatehouse is the Tavistock Canal, on either side of which are many mid-nineteenth-century industrial cottages erected by the Duke of Bedford for the miners who flocked into the area with the copper boom, a good example of a socially enlightened housing policy.

• MORWELLHAM •

Mention has been made of the Tavistock Canal and the nineteenth-century copper boom. This brings the West Devon story neatly to Morwellham (the accent is on the last syllable), a place with a story. There had been a port of sorts at Morwellham for hundreds of years prior to the copper boom of the 1790s. This was the nearest point on the river to Tavistock which sea-going ships could reach, but trade was desultory.

Although, as the proverbial crow flies, Morwellham is only 3 miles (5km) from Tavistock, by road the distance is nearer 5 miles (8km), and the 600ft (210m) obstacle of Morwell Down lies between, as well as the valley of the River Lumburn, no small

Morwellham Quay

impediments in the days of horse transport and poor roads. So, when copper was discovered at Wheal Friendship, a mine at Mary Tavy north of Tavistock, in the 1790s, an efficient way of exporting it to the South Wales smelting works had to be devised.

The canal was started in 1803, and simultaneously work began at each end of the tunnel. To achieve quicker progress, a series of shafts was sunk so that several faces could be worked at once. Even so, the tunnel took 14 years to complete. In the meantime, the canal had been finished from Tavistock to Creber, where the tunnel began, and was in use to that point by 1809.

For 27 years Morwellham was moderately prosperous, and then in 1844 much larger quantities of copper were found 5 miles (8km) north at Blanchdown. The canal passed nowhere near it, so a standard gauge railway was constructed in 1858 to the top of the hill above the port and a second, larger, inclined plane built alongside the one servicing the canal.

After 20 years of continuous working, the copper lodes began to be exhausted but arsenic, hitherto little regarded, was now suddenly in demand for various commercial and agricultural uses. So, arsenic roasting furnaces and flues were built, and thousands of tons exported but by 1901 the mines were abandoned. The canal was closed in 1872, never having been able to compete with the railway.

Morwellham quietly mouldered away. The docks silted up and became choked with weeds.

The tiled quays were stolen, and the inn lost its licence. However, the canal was revived in 1933 to bring water to the Morwellham hydro-electric station.

Then in 1970 Morwellham had life breathed into it again, when work began to restore its buildings, equipment and docks. It became **Morwellham Quay** with trails, museums, a shop, restaurant and most exciting of all, a trip underground after a riverside train ride to see what conditions were really like. Morwellham is now bustling with activity again.

Morwellham Quay

Off A390, 5 miles west of Tavistock. Riverside village restored and brought back to life. Craft demonstrations. Try on Victorian costumes. Tour a copper mine on a real mine railway. Visit the Secret Valley and Tamar Valley Wildlife Reserve with bird hides and magnificent views. Shops and restaurants. ☎ 01822 832766. Open: all year, daily 10am–5.30pm (closed 23 December to 3 January inclusive). 4.30pm closing November to Easter. Last admission 2 hours before closing. Many facilities subject to seasonal opening only.

Dartmoor – Northern Area

4

If the main holiday area in Devon is centred on Torquay, and visitors tend to come to Dartmoor while on holiday, then the approach through Newton Abbot and Bovey Tracey (pronounced 'Buvvy') is a natural one, and will be the starting point for a figure-of-eight journey across and around the moor. This chapter describes the area in the north of the figure, and the next chapter that in the south. It helps to have a basic understanding of Dartmoor's shape; two upland plateaux, separated by two roads bisecting each other like a pair of scissors at Two Bridges.

Drive carefully past the ponies on Dartmoor and do not feed them!

• BOVEY TRACEY •

The name Bovey refers to the river which passes through the parish, and the second element connects it with the de Tracey family, one of whose members, Sir William de Tracey, was in the party which murdered Thomas à Becket in Canterbury Cathedral in 1170.

Riverside Mill

Bovey Tracey. Display of ceramics, jewellery, prints, furniture, textiles etc. Touring exhibitions. Shop and Egon Ronay listed café. ☎ 01626 832223. Open daily (except winter bank holidays), 10am–5.30pm.

The church is very beautiful, with a fine rood screen and carved stone pulpit, while the Riverside Mill is now home to a number of craftsmen of the Devon Guild of Craftsmen.

To the south of the town, towards the Drum Bridges roundabout on the A38, the **House of Marbles** and **Teign Valley Glassworks** gives visitors the opportunity of watching glassmaking, as well as having probably the biggest collection of marbles in the world.

Nearby can be found **Cardew Teapottery**, a pottery entirely devoted to the making of teapots. One of the attractions is the activity area where visitors of all ages can try their hand at making or decorating a teapot.

At the other end of the town is **Parke**, the headquarters of the Dartmoor National Park Authority. The house and estate were left to the National Trust by Major Hole, on his death in 1974. The house was built on the site of an older building by the major's grandfather in the 1820s. The Trust leases the house to the National Park Authority.

In 1951, Dartmoor was declared a national park. This designation did not alter the status of the land: the moor remains in private ownership. It means that all developments are looked at very carefully by the planning authority, the Dartmoor National Park Authority. This body also has a duty to help the public enjoy the park. This is achieved through information and interpretative services, guided walks, the erection of signposts, stiles and foot bridges, subsidised bus services and a team of rangers out on the moor making contact with residents and visitors.

A joint National Park and National Trust information centre is incorporated in the

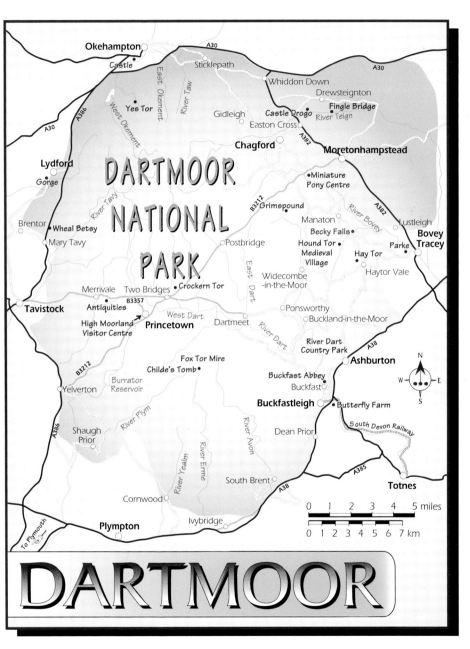

Okehampton
Castle
Sticklepath
A30
Whiddon Down
A30
Drewsteignton
East Okement
River Taw
Yes Tor
Gidleigh
Castle Drogo
Easton Cross
Fingle Bridge
River Teign
West Okement
A386
A30
Chagford
A382
Moretonhampstead
Lydford
Gorge
DARTMOOR
NATIONAL
PARK
Miniature
Pony Centre
River Tavy
B3212
Grimspound
Manaton
River Bovey
Lustleigh
Brentor
Wheal Betsy
Mary Tavy
Becky Falls
Hound Tor
Medieval
Village
Parke
Bovey
Tracey
A382
Postbridge
Hay Tor
Haytor Vale
East Dart
Widecombe
-in-the-Moor
Merrivale
Two Bridges
Crockern Tor
Tavistock
Antiquities
B3357
West Dart
High Moorland
Visitor Centre
Princetown
Dartmeet
River Dart
Ponsworthy
Buckland-in-the-Moor
River Dart
Country Park
Ashburton
A38
N
W
E
S
Fox Tor Mire
Childe's Tomb
B3212
Burrator
Reservoir
Buckfast Abbey
Buckfast
Buckfastleigh
Butterfly Farm
Yelverton
River Plym
Dean Prior
South Devon Railway
Shaugh
Prior
A386
River Yealm
River Erme
River Avon
South Brent
A38
A385
Totnes
Cornwood
Ivybridge
0 1 2 3 4 5 miles
0 1 2 3 4 5 6 7 km
To Plymouth
Plympton

DARTMOOR

buildings and there are lovely riverside walks on the estate.

Beyond Parke, the road divides at a stone direction post at Five

Wyches Cross, where you should fork to the left and climb steadily for $3\frac{1}{2}$ miles (5.5km) to the car park near **Hay Tor**. Hay Tor is

The deserted medieval village at Hound Tor, Dartmoor

without doubt the most noticed, most recognised and most visited tor on Dartmoor. On one side the land falls away; on the other the open moor rolls into the distance — there is no better viewpoint from which to get one's Dartmoor bearings.

A few hundred yards to the north-east is a large quarry boasting a pool where goldfish lurk, saved from predatory herons by the depth of the water. A cutting leads from the lower quarry, and if this is followed, a double line of grooved stone blocks will be seen bearing round to the left beside a tip of waste rock. This is the **Hay Tor granite tramway.**

Between 1825 and 1858 stone was transported from this quarry and others nearby, on flat-top horse-drawn, wooden-wheeled trucks for 8 miles (13km), down a tramway built of continuous lines of these grooved sets. The enterprise supplied stone for many London buildings, including parts of London Bridge and the British Museum Library before becoming uneconomic due to the high cost of transportation.

A walk of discovery

The stone tramway is visible for much of its course on the moor, and to follow it makes an easy and fascinating walk of discovery. The 'points' in particular are of the greatest interest. Of course, the system reverses the usual railway practice of having the flange on the wheels. Here the flange was on the 'rails', and the trucks' wheels were plain wood with iron hoops.

If the walk is extended past **Great Tor** to **Hound Tor** the interesting remains of a deserted medieval village can be explored. Enclosures, houses, including what was probably a small manor house, and corn-drying kilns can be recognised. By the fourteenth century the climate had deteriorated, so that farming on these bleak moors was not practical, and the settlement was abandoned. Alternatively by parking at the Hound Tor car park and walking the short distance past the tor the site can be clearly seen.

• WIDECOMBE-IN-THE-MOOR •

After looking round the area, carry on towards Widecombe-in-the-Moor, 4 miles (6km) or so further on. Over the top of Widecombe Hill, an enormous panorama is spread out in front. Southern Dartmoor and northern Dartmoor are recognisable, joined by the high saddle of North Hessary Tor beyond Princetown, this summit surmounted by a 700ft (245m) BBC television mast. The long whale-back hill 'behind' Widecombe is Hameldon.

Widecombe's rise to fame as a result of the popularity of the famous song 'Widecombe Fair' is probably due to the shrewd commercial sense of those who would profit from it. The song was first written down and popularised in the 1880s, when Widecombe Fair was in its infancy, and of course the individuals mentioned in the chorus — Bill Brewer, Jan Stewer, Peter Gurney, Peter Davy, Dan'l Whiddon, Harry Hawk, Old Uncle Tom Cobley and all — were all going to the fair from somewhere else.

Widecombe-in-the-Moor is a very popular tourist village, made famous by the song 'Widecombe Fair'

The ancient clapper bridge at Dartmeet

When the fair began, it was what we would now call a market, with some revelling for good measure. Now, it is more of a gymkhana, with a sheep, cattle and pony show, demonstrations, competitions, sideshows, races and refreshments. It is held on the second Tuesday in September, and attracts thousands of people.

• THE CENTRAL AREA •

Dartmeet is a famous beauty spot where the East and West Dart Rivers come together among magnificent scenery. Just upstream from the road bridge are the flood-damaged remains of an ancient clapper bridge.

For many people, **Two Bridges** is the centre of Dartmoor, though a glance at a map of the National Park will show that Bellever Forest has more precise claims to that distinction. The Rivers Cowsic and West Dart come together here, and a five-span clapper bridge on the Cowsic may be one of the original 'Two Bridges', the one over the West Dart having disappeared.

Back at the road, continue towards Tavistock, taking the right fork after crossing the West Dart. **Dartmoor Prison** comes into view (left) and the road passes through prison farmland. The prison is virtually self-supporting so far as meat and vegetables are concerned.

• THE WESTERN SIDE, LYDFORD •

Pass through Merrivale and, at Tavistock, turn right and follow the A386 north to Mary Tavy where you should take the turning left signposted Brent Tor. Drive to the car park below the church-crowned tor, which gives its name to the village, and walk up the path to the summit by the longer, but less steep, way. The view from the top is one of the finest in England.

A clear day will enable you to see right into the inner recesses of northern Dartmoor, where Fur Tor and Cut Hill stand out. Even Exmoor appears as a blue blur to the north. The tiny church was built in 1130 and stands 1,130ft above sea level, a useful conjunction of numerals. Burials have taken place up to the present time, and one marvels that a sufficient depth of soil exists for the purpose.

Now take the road signposted to Lydford, a small village, but a vast parish, about 4 miles (6.7km) north-east. **Lydford** is superficially a very unprepossessing village, with none of the thatched-roof cosiness of eastern Dartmoor. The small castle dominates one end of the single street, it is true, but the fascinating story of Lydford has to be sought out, and the casual, uninformed, visitor could miss a great deal.

The village's situation was its *raison d'être*. **The deep gorge** of the River Lyd blocks the approach on one side, with a secondary valley forming the other. King Alfred adapted these natural advantages by raising an earth bank across the third side,

to create Lydford, one of his four strategically-placed *burghs* or fortified positions in Devon against the Danes.

A mint was established, and it became an important local centre. It never developed to any extent, and was overtaken by Okehampton and Launceston, which lay on the main route through the south-west peninsula, and by Tavistock, with its abbey. For this reason, Lydford's ancient road pattern has not been overlaid by later building. Some of the original Saxon plots and lanes laid out on a grid model can be seen, as well as Alfred's earthbank.

Soon after the Norman Conquest, the invaders re-fortified the site by building a fort on a corner overlooking one of the steep slopes, but this had a short life, as **the castle** dates from about 1195.

Beside the castle is Lydford church, dedicated to a Celtic saint, St Petrock, which gives credence to the suggestion that there may once have been a Celtic community here. The font is the oldest feature in the church, and the screen is a splendid example of modern (1904) craftsmanship.

At the bottom of the hill below the church is **Lydford Gorge** (National Trust), down which rushes the River Lyd. In places 200ft (70m) deep with 60ft (21m) vertical walls at the bottom, the gorge has been formed by the urgent passage of the river carrying rocks which have scoured out potholes along its course.

Lydford Gorge

The Stables, Lydford. Exciting path along the ravine leads to the whirlpool known as the Devil's Cauldron. Over a mile (2km) along the gorge is a 100ft waterfall, White Lady, the highest on Dartmoor. Circular walk takes in both spectacles. Arduous walk unsuitable for disabled visitors. Shop and tearoom (April to October and weekends November and December). ☎ 01822 820441/820320. Open: April to October, daily 10am–5.30pm. Limited access November to March, daily 10.30am–3pm.

Much of the course of the gorge is truly awe inspiring and a little frightening, and other parts are very beautiful. If you visit Lydford in the winter, when for safety's sake the gorge is closed, the flavour of the place can be felt by looking over Lydford Bridge into the deepest section.

Pass through Lydford and rejoin the A386 at the Dartmoor Inn, turning left, and heading for Okehampton. The high moor is very near the road along here, and by glancing right you will see the prominent stone cross on Brat Tor erected in 1887 to mark Queen Victoria's silver jubilee. A few miles on, turn right towards **Okehampton**, getting a glimpse of Dartmoor's highest tor, Yes Tor 2,030ft (619m), if it is unobscured by cloud.

• OKEHAMPTON •

The dramatic ruin of Baron Baldwin's Norman castle on the right down a winding tree-lined road into the town is the great attraction of Okehampton. The castle was built along a narrow ridge, with ancillary buildings leading up the slope from the barbican to the keep. Garderobes — medieval lavatories — are built into the outside walls to take advantage of the slope. On a fine spring day, when the bluebells are blooming in bud-bursting time, with the chorale of the nearby West Okement River as background music, fairyland seems to have come to mid-Devon.

Okehampton Castle

Take side road by the Post Office. Largest medieval castle in Devon. Free personal audio tour. Special events.
☎ 01837 52844.
Open: April to October, daily from 10am.

The distinguished town hall in Fore Street was built in 1685, as a private house for John Northmore, and converted to its present use in 1821. The **Museum of Dartmoor Life**, on the opposite side of the road, reveals how people lived and worked in the area for hundreds of years.

The model railway museum at the former station at Okehampton

Before leaving the town spare some time to visit The **Oke-hampton Railway Station Visitor Centre,** a restored working Southern Railway station. During the summer, passenger services to and from Exeter terminate here, linked to vintage and modern bus services.

Museum of Dartmoor Life

3 West Street, Okehampton. Working water wheel. Interactive exhibits. Temporary exhibitions. Gift and book shop. Tearoom and information centre.
☎ 01837 52295. Open: April, May and October, Monday to Saturday 10am–4pm. June to September, daily 10am–4pm. November to March, Monday to Friday, 10am–4pm.

Okehampton Visitor Centre

Station Road. Museum and model railway. Special events.
Restaurant. Gift shop and model shop. ☎ 01837 55330.
Open: May to October, daily 9.30am–5.30pm. November to April,
Wednesday to Sunday 10.30am–4.30pm.

• THE NORTH-EAST •

About 4 miles (6km) east of Okehampton is Sticklepath,
a village frequently visited by John Wesley.

In the centre of Sticklepath is the **Finch Foundry Museum of Waterpower**. From 1814 to 1960 agricultural equipment was made here by Heath Robinson-type machinery, powered by water from the Taw. After closure, a band of interested people preserved the machinery which is now shown to the public. It was given to the National Trust in 1993.

Finch Foundry Museum of Waterpower

Sticklepath, 4 miles east of
Okehampton. Regular
demonstrations of working water
wheels, forge with huge tilt
hammers and grindstone.
Disabled access difficult. Shop
and tearoom. ☎ 01837 840046.
Open: April to October, daily
except Tuesday 11am–5.30pm.

*The Square at Chagford
with its Market House*

Head eastwards from Sticklepath, and fork right at Whiddon Down, along the A382 as far as Easton Cross. Take the right turn here to **Chagford**. The name means gorse ford, although the town stands well above the beautiful River Teign, here crossed by a lengthy line of stepping stones known as Rushford Steps, over which sacks of grain were carried to **Rushford Mill**.

Facing the church is the sixteenth-century Three Crowns Inn, with jutting porch, where a young cavalier, Sidney Godolphin, was killed in a Civil War skirmish. The centre of the town is remarkable for its sense of focus. All roads lead to the Square, with its 1862 market house and comprehensive range of shops.

• CASTLE DROGO •

An expedition from Chagford must be to Castle Drogo (National Trust) at **Drewsteignton**, which is often described as the last great country house which will ever be built in England.

Julius Drewe, the original owner, made his money from the Home and Colonial Stores. Believing there to be a link between his family and the Norman Drogo (or Dru) de Teigne who gave his name to Drewsteignton, he bought land in the parish and set his heart on a castle. Mr (later Sir) Edwin Lutyens was recommended to him and he began work on Drewe's romantic dream of reproducing a twentieth-century version of an all-granite medieval castle.

Work proceeded exceedingly slowly, albeit on a scaled-down version of the first design, and the two original masons of 1911 eventually finished the castle in 1930. Sadly, Julius Drewe died a year later. The origin of Drewe's fortune was not forgotten and local people disrespectfully chris-

The granite-built Castle Drogo designed by Lutyens. It is now owned by The National Trust

Part of the Castle Drogo garden

tened his house 'Margarine Castle'. Even in its reduced size, Castle Drogo is massive in scale, and inconvenient for modern living.

Castle Drogo

Near Drewsteignton. 20th-century granite castle commanding spectacular views of Dartmoor. Elegant interior, formal gardens and fine walks on the estate. Children's playground. Shop and plant centre, restaurant and tearoom. Limited disabled access to part of castle. ☎ 01647 433306. Open: April to October, daily except Friday 11am–5.30pm (open Good Friday). Gardens open April to October daily, 10.30am–5.30pm.

It would be wrong to leave the neighbourhood without visiting **Fingle Bridge**, a well known, but unspoilt, beauty spot, 2 miles (3km) away on the other side of Drewsteignton. Here the River Teign sparkles beneath the 400-year-old stone bridge, among beautiful wooded hills. A licensed restaurant, the Anglers' Rest, stands at the foot of Prestonbury, which has an Iron Age hillfort on its summit.

Public footpaths lead up and downstream, and the most beguiling, the **Hunters' Path**, climbs up through the oak woods to come out above the tree line, with the spectacle of expansive views ahead to northern Dartmoor. As Castle Drogo can be reached by turning off the Hunters' Path, this route provides a most pleasant link between the two places.

Turning south, the small town of **Moretonhampstead,** at the junction of the A382 and B3212, should be visited. The town is notable for the fine arcaded stone almshouses, dated 1637, in Cross Street.

From Moretonhampstead it is a straightforward drive back to the starting point of this exploration of the northern area of Dartmoor, leaving the southern area for another day.

Dartmoor – Southern Area

The exploration of the southern area of Dartmoor can also begin at Bovey Tracey and an interesting day's outing (or several days) can be enjoyed without retracing the journeys made in the previous chapter.

Follow the A382 north, or the network of minor roads to the west of it, to reach the B3212. Three miles west of Moretonhampstead is the **Miniature Pony Centre** which offers a day out on Dartmoor with something for all the family.

Miniature Pony Centre

Nr Moretonhampstead. Hands-on 'kids' farmyard, nature trails, craft centre, pony rides, indoor and outdoor adventure play areas. Shop and courtyard café. ☎ 01647 432400. Open: Easter to November, daily 10.30am–4.30pm (later when busy).

The granite tramway at Hay Tor

Beyond, the road leads, after a further 2 miles (3km), to a steep climb onto the open moor at Moorgate Hill. The first turning left after reaching the moor leads to **Grimspound**, a prehistoric village settlement. Grimspound lies 300yd (274m) east of the minor road 1$^1/_2$ miles (2km) south of the B3212 at **Challacombe Cross**. Although some of the ruined huts at Grimspound have been 'restored' or built up, and as most of the huts on the moor are not so recognisable, it is a good introduction to similar antiquities.

At Grimspound a ruined stone wall encloses an area of nearly 4 acres (1.5hectares) in which archaeologists found the remains of twenty-four huts, as well as what may have been cattle pens built against the wall. The paved entrance is on the higher side and gave access to the pastures on Hameldon, the high ground to the south.

After the secod switchback, the road levels out; beside the road on the south side is the leaning and misshapen **Bennett's Cross**.

The next building to the west is the **Warren House Inn**, which once served the miners from the tin mines below the road. The deep gashes show where they followed the east-west striking tin lodes. Work went on here until earlier this century.

Postbridge is like an oasis in the middle of the moor, with beech trees instead of palms. The finest clapper bridge on the moor is easily seen a few yards down stream from the road bridge.

Carrying on towards Prince-town, about 1 mile (1.5km) west of Postbridge, on the north side of the road, are the ruins of a nineteenth-century gunpowder factory, known as the **Powder Mills**. Here the three constituents of that compound were brought together — the charcoal at least was provided by locally-grown timber — and the various processes powered by water from the East Dart River. The safety factor of space was available in abundance, and batches of powder were tested by firing a proving mortar, which still stands near the cottages.

Princetown came into being through the prison which was started in 1806 on land owned by the Prince of Wales. The prison was built by French prisoners of war, who had hitherto been incarcerated in overcrowded hulks at Plymouth, and later Americans joined the French within the walls: at one time there were 7,000 men held captive, with 500 soldiers guarding them. Initially it was referred to as the War Prison or Depot.

The oldest building in the area is the **Plume of Feathers**, a slate-hung hostelry dating from before the prison. In 1993 Prince Charles opened the splendid **High Moorland Visitor Centre** in the one-time Duchy Hotel, and this is the best place to find out about the national park under one roof.

Beyond Princetown the road once again crosses open moor, and the track of the Princetown branch railway (closed 1956) can be seen on the right. The road also passes close to several hut circles.

• THE SOUTHERN FRINGE •

The first turning on the left after leaving the open moor leads (by either road at a fork) to Burrator Reservoir, by far the most beautiful reservoir on Dartmoor. It was built in 1898 to solve Plymouth's water problems and increased in size in 1928.

From the dam the foothill lanes bring one, via Meavy and Cadover Bridge, to Shaugh Bridge, below the village of **Shaugh Prior**. From the car park beside the bridge, a delightful 2-mile (3km) walk on National Trust land to the top of the Dewerstone through woods, along a quarry tramway and up to the breezy summit. This is the Trust's Goodameavy estate; it also owns a stretch of Wigford Down, a landscape peppered with prehistoric remains.

From Shaugh Bridge, head south-eastwards through Cornwood to Ivybridge from where the A38 dual carriageway can be followed as far as **South Brent**. This little town has a number of pleasant buildings, especially the Toll House with its list of charges, and the church. Originally a cruciform Norman building with a central tower, at some stage the west end was demolished.

• BUCKFASTLEIGH & ASHBURTON •

Buckfastleigh was formerly a wool town which derived its power from the River Mardle. Diversification has come to Buckfastleigh, however, and many different ventures now thrive in the little town where the moor meets the South Hams. The spired church, rare on Dartmoor but burnt out in the early 1990s, stands aloof from the town on a nearby hill.

In the churchyard is a curious mausoleum-like structure erected over Richard Cabell's tomb following his death in 1677, to make sure his unquiet spirit could not escape to haunt the neighbourhood, since he was thought to be in league with the devil. Tales of fire-breathing black dogs howling round his tomb were adapted by

Conan Doyle when he was researching for *The Hound of the Baskervilles*.

Newcomers to Devon will visit the area chiefly to see Buckfast Abbey and the South Devon (the old Dart Valley) Railway, and the two are conveniently sited only about half a mile apart. Just across the A38 from the town is Pennywell Farm where children can meet not only farm animals, but small mammals, falcons and owls. ☎ 01364 642023. Open: Easter to October, daily 10am–5.00pm.

A monastic community lived at Buckfast from before the Norman Conquest to 1539 when, with the dissolution of the monasteries, the buildings were abandoned and fell into decay. In 1882 a band of French monks acquired the site, and in 1907 the abbot decided to rebuild. The only resources available at that time were £1, a horse and cart, and much faith; none of the monks had any knowledge of building techniques. The decision made, one of the monks left Buckfast to learn the basic skills of masonry, and on his return the work went ahead, but with never more than six brothers working at the same time. The **Buckfast Abbey** that we see today was finished exactly thirty years later.

To make the monastery financially self-supporting, many activities are carried on by the monks. Dartmoor heather provides the raw material for honey, tonic wine of secret formula and cider are also made, cattle and poultry are kept, and the kitchen gardens are carefully cultivated. Other monks, more skilful with their hands, produce works of art in pottery, stained glass, painting, illumination and carving. All of them do what they can for the good of the community.

Buckfast Abbey

Buckfast. Exhibition of the history of the Abbey, surviving medieval buildings, video presentation, Physic Garden and Pleasure Garden. Grange Restaurant. Monastic Produce Shop, Gift Shop, Abbey Bookshop. ☎ 01364 642519. Church and Grounds Open: All year, daily 5.30am–7pm. Services are held daily and all are open to the public. Visitor Facilities Open: April to October, daily 9am–5.30pm, November to March, daily 10am–4pm. On Sundays the shops open at 12noon.

The **South Devon Railway** runs along the old Ashburton line on Great Western Railway principles, from Buckfastleigh to Staverton, and on to Totnes. Here the locomotives have to change ends and pull trains back to Buckfastleigh. Many films and television serials have used the railway to achieve period atmosphere.

Opposite page: Buckfast Abbey

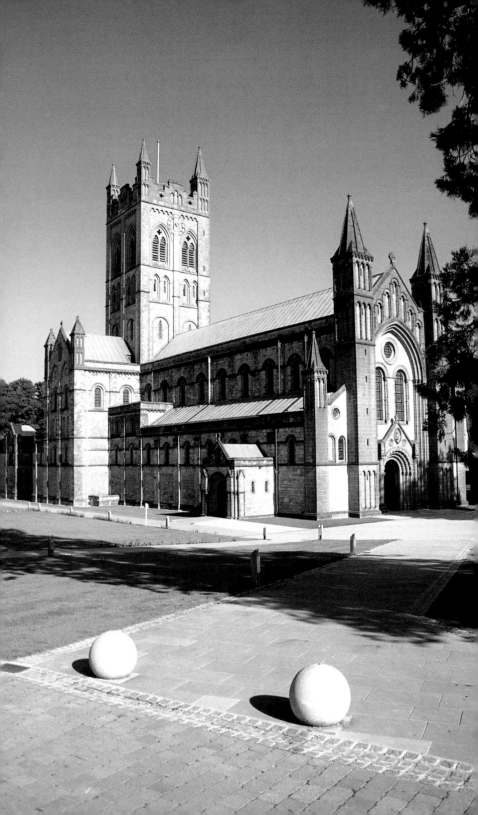

South Devon Railway

Buckfastleigh. Steam trains run for 7 miles along the east bank of the River Dart. Shop, museum, model railway and café at Buckfastleigh Station. Special events during the year. ☎ 01364 642338. Open: mid-March to end of October, daily during school holidays and summer season, weekends and some weekdays at other times. Santa specials near Christmas. ☎ for details of exact timetable.

of the Mermaid Inn, now an iron-monger's shop, where General Fairfax stayed in 1646 during the Civil War.

Ashburton Museum

West Street, Ashburton. Displays of local history and internationally-renowned North American Indian collection. ☎ 01364 653426. Open: Mid-May to late September, Tuesday, Thursday, Friday, Saturday, 2.30–5pm.

Ashburton, Buckfastleigh's twin, lies 2$^1/_2$ miles (4km) away up the A38, a pleasant little town with many attractive houses, shops and interesting corners. It repays a leisurely visit. The slate-hung front elevations are locally distinctive. In the centre of the town is a Gothic arch on the site

From Ashburton, 1$^1/_2$ miles (2km) up the Two Bridges road is the **River Dart Country Park**. Here is something for every-one: a privately run riverside park in beautiful grounds beside the tree-lined River Dart. Children, especially, love the sylvan spaciousness.

Buckfast Butterflies & Dartmoor Otter Sanctuary

Buckfastleigh. Otter feeding times 11.30am, 2.00pm and 4.30pm. ☎ 01364 642916. Open: April to October 10am–5.30pm or dusk.

River Dart Country Park

Holne Park, Ashburton. Walks, lakes, tennis, riding stables, swimming pool and adventure playground. Licensed restaurant and tea garden. Shop. ☎ 01364 652511.
Open: Easter/1st April to end of September, daily 10am–5pm.

• NORTH OF ASHBURTON •

Buckland-in-the-Moor is a tiny village high up above the Dart, and reached by a signposted turning right beyond the country park. The moorstone church of St Peter is beautifully situated on a hillside, overlooking the deep and wooded valley but it is chiefly visited to see the tower clock, which has letters reading MY DEAR MOTHER instead of numerals.

Buckland Beacon is one of the best viewpoints on Dartmoor. Between the church and the Beacon is a well kept group of thatched stone cottages, which seem to have come to life from a chocolate box. This is probably the single most photographed scene on the moor.

Drive on to a T-junction, turn right and $1^1/_2$ miles (2km) further on, at the bleak crossroads known as Cold East Cross, turn left. Carry straight on at Hemsworthy Gate and make for Manaton, past **Hound Tor** (right), one of Dartmoor's finest tors.

Through **Manaton,** with a tree-shaded green near the church, in the direction of Bovey Tracey are **Becky Falls.** These are well worth a visit after heavy rain as the falls then have something to show while in dry weather the boulders, which form the cataract, conceal the stream. The oak woodland is particularly beautiful in spring and autumn.

Becky Falls

Manaton. River walks, discovery trails, waterfalls. Restaurant and tearoom. Gift shop. Picnic area.
☎ 01647 221259.
Open: Mid-March to early November, daily 10am–6pm (or dusk if earlier).

The road towards Bovey Tracey winds vertiginously over Trendlebere Down, a moor-edge eminence giving expansive views eastwards. Leaving the moor, and just after the cattle grid, a turning right leads into **Yarner Wood,** where the Nature Conservancy Council has laid out two nature trails, one short, one longer.

HOW TO GET TO SOUTH DEVON

By Car

M4/M5 or M25/M3/A303/A30 to Exeter. A38 Devon Expressway links Exeter to Plymouth with access to all destinations in between.

By Rail

Direct services from London (Paddington), the Midlands, North of England, South Wales and Scotland. Contact National Rail Enquiry Office ☎ 0345 484950 for further details, or website, www.rail.co.uk/ukrail/home.htm

By Coach

National Express runs regular services to South Devon from most areas of Britain. ☎ 0990 808080 for details or website, http://www.eurolines.co.uk

By Air

Direct flights to Plymouth or Exeter from Cork, Jersey, Guernsey, Paris and London Gatwick. Connecting flights from other UK destinations. Contact British Airways for further details, ☎ 0345 222111 or website, www.british-airways.co.uk

By Sea

To Plymouth from Roscoff, Brittany and Santander, Spain. Contact Brittany Ferries, ☎ 0990 360360 (Plymouth); ☎ (298) 292800 (Roscoff); ☎ (942) 220000 (Santander) or website, www.brittany-ferries.co.uk/home.htm

ACCOMMODATION

There is a very wide range of accommodation available throughout the area, from hotels, guest-houses, farmhouses, bed and breakfast establishments, inns and youth hostels, to caravan and camp sites, self-catering in all types of property and camping barns.

Hotels, Guest Houses, Bed and Breakfast, Inns

Details of this type of accommodation can be obtained from the appropriate local Tourist Information Centre. These are listed towards the end of the FactFile.

The Dartmoor Tourist Association issues a comprehensive guide to both serviced and self-catering accommodation in the Dartmoor area, ☎ 01822 890567 or write to Dartmoor Tourist Association, The Duchy Building, Tavistock Road, Princetown, PL20 6QF.

Farm Holidays

Cream of West Devon Farm Holiday Group,
Helen Alford   ☎ 01837 861381
Farm Holiday Bureau, Linda Harvey   ☎ 01626 833266
West Devon Friendly Farm Holiday Group, Jane Pyle   ☎ 01363 82510

Youth Hostels

Details of YHA hostels in the area from **Youth Hostels Association**, Via Gellia Mill, Bonsall, Matlock, Derbys.

Caravan and Camp Sites

Devon County Council produces a leaflet *DEVON Self-catering Holiday Parks, Caravan and Camping* which may be obtained from Devon Tourist Information Centre, Exeter Services, Sidmouth Road, Exeter, EX2 7HF, ☎ 01392 437581 or e-mail ahopkins@mf.devon-cc.gov.uk

Self-Catering

Local Tourist Information Centres and the following agencies will be pleased to supply details of properties available or contact Devon TIC as above:

Dartmoor and South Devon Farm and Country Holidays,	☎ 01364 621391
Devon Connection,	☎ 01548 560964 or website www.devonconnection.co.uk
Helpful Holidays,	☎ 01647 433593
Salcombe Holiday Homes,	☎ 01548 843485 or website www.salcombe.co.uk

Camping Barns

There are a number of camping barns on Dartmoor. For details ☎ 01271 324420.

Specialist Holidays

For details of "Activity Holidays, Learning Holidays and Event Packages" contact **Economy and Tourism**, Exeter City Council, Civic Centre, Paris Street, Exeter, EX1 1JJ. ☎ 01392 265900.

'Last Minute' Bookings

Contact the Devon TIC, ☎ 01392 437581 or e-mail ahopkins@mf.devon-cc.gov.uk Give details of the location, type and price range of the accommodation being sought and they will try to find what is wanted and make the booking.

BIRD WATCHING SITES

Berry Head Country Park, Brixham; **Dawlish Warren**, east of Dawlish; **Exe Estuary**, reserves on east and west shores; **Fernworthy Reservoir**, approx. 6 miles west of Moretenhampstead; **Prawle Point**, south of Kingsbridge; **Slapton Ley Nature Reserve**, nr Torcross; **Yarner Wood**, between Bovey Tracey and Manaton.

CYCLING

Devon County Council publishes details of a number of cycling routes in South Devon covering long and short distances and including some off-road routes. Contact Devon Tourist Information Centre, Exeter Services, Sidmouth Road, Exeter, EX2 7HF, ☎ 01392 437581, for a free leaflet *Now You're Really Cycling* outlining the routes. A detailed itinerary for each route can be purchased from the same address.

Dartmoor National Park Authority publishes a guide to cycling on Dartmoor and three leaflets (£1.00 each) showing suitable off-road routes. They are available from all National Park Information Centres or ☎ 01822 890414.

Cycling is only allowed on public roads, byways open to all traffic, public bridlepaths and Forestry Commission roads. Cycling is not permitted on public footpaths, common land or open moorland.

FACILITIES FOR THE DISABLED

Entries in this guide include information about facilities for the disabled where this is known.

The English Riviera Tourist Board publishes a free leaflet *Information for the Disabled,* which details facilities, specialist equipment hire, transport, hotels, restaurants, tourist attractions, car parking etc and also local organisations and associations which can offer help and advice. Contact the Tourist Centre, Vaughan Parade, Torquay, TQ2 5JG, ☎ 01803 296296 or e-mail tourist.board@torbay.gov.uk or website www.torbay.gov.uk

For information on accessible areas on Dartmoor there is a leaflet *Easygoing Dartmoor* available from local information centres or ☎ 01822 890414.

FERRIES

Dartmouth to Kingswear. Operates all year, approximately every 10 minutes, vehicles and passengers.

Salcombe/East Portlemouth Ferry, ☎ 01548 842061. Runs all year to and from Salcombe and East Portlemouth.

South Sands Ferry, ☎ 01548 561035. Runs South Sands to Salcombe between Easter and the end of October half-term.

Western Lady Ferry Service, ☎ 01803 852041 (Brixham) and 01803 297292. Runs from Torquay to Brixham and return, May to 2nd or 3rd week in October; daily in July, August and September, not Saturdays in May, June and October.

Details of other ferry services that are useful when walking the coastal paths may be found in the South West Way Association guide, ☎ 01803 873061.

GOLF

There are several golf courses in the area which accept non-members on payment of green fees. A selection only is given here.

Ashbury Golf Course, Okehampton — ☎ 01837 55453

Bigbury Golf Course, nr Salcombe — ☎ 01548 810207

Dartmouth Golf and Country Club — ☎ 01803 712686

Dainton Park, Newton Abbott — ☎ 01803 813812

Teign Valley Golf Club — ☎ 01647 253026

Teignmouth Golf Club — ☎ 01626 772894

Torquay Golf Club — ☎ 01803 327471

Wrangaton Golf Club, nr South Brent — ☎ 01364 73229.

GUIDED CITY TOURS

Exeter City Council Red Coat Guides offer free guided walks around the City, on a variety of themes, between April and October. Most walks last $1^1/_2$ hours and there are between 4 and 6 a day to choose from. Between November and March there is a reduced programme of 2 tours per day (1 on Sunday, afternoon only).

☎ 01392 265212 for full details.

GUIDED WALKS

Dartmoor National Park Authority offers a programme of guided walks from Easter to mid-October. They vary from gentle $1^1/_2$ hour strolls to full days on the high moors. All walks have a theme whether it be wildlife, archaeology, sketching, navigation skills, strolls by moonlight or picnic walks. A small charge is made for participants unless they arrive by public transport (ticket to be shown to walk leader) in which case the walk is FREE. Full programme available from local Tourist Information Centres and published in *DARTMOOR VISITOR*, the annual free information newspaper issued by the Park Authority. ☎ 01822 890414 for further information.

HORSE RIDING

There are a number of riding stables in the area, offering everything from a short, gentle beginner's trek to a full-day excursion. A selection only is listed below.

Babeny Farm Riding Stables,
  Dartmeet, — ☎ 01364 631296
Cholwell Riding Stables,
  Mary Tavy, — ☎ 01822 810526
Cockington Riding Stables,
  Torquay, — ☎ 01803 606860

Littlecombe Riding Centre, Holne, nr Ashburton,	☎ 01364 631260
Lydford House Riding Stables, Lydford,	☎ 01822 820321
Moorland Riding Stables, Mary Tavy,	☎ 01822 810293
Primley Riding Stables, Paignton,	☎ 01803 557222
River Dart Country Park, Ashburton,	☎ 01364 652511
Sherberton Stables, Hexworthy, nr Dartmeet,	☎ 01364 631276
Shilstone Rocks Riding Centre, Widecombe-in-the-Moor,	☎ 01364 621281
Skaigh Stables, Sticklepath,	☎ 01837 840429

MAPS

The following Ordnance Survey maps cover the area included in this book:

Explorer Series, 1:25 000 scale (4cm to 1km or $2^1/_2$in to 1 mile).
108 *Lower Tamar Valley and Plymouth*; 110 *Torquay and Dawlish*;
114 *Exeter and the Exe Valley*

Outdoor Leisure Series, 1:25 000 scale (4cm to 1km or $2^1/_2$in to 1 mile)
20 *South Devon - Brixham to Newton Ferrers*; 28 *Dartmoor*

Landranger Series, 1: 50 000 scale (2cm to 1km or $1^1/_4$in to 1 mile)
191 *Okehampton and North Dartmoor*; 192 *Exeter and Sidmouth*
201 *Plymouth and Launceston, Tavistock and Looe*; 202 *Torbay and
South Dartmoor, Totnes and Salcombe*

PUBLIC TRANSPORT

There is an increasing network of public transport throughout the area,
enabling visitors to travel in comfort without the strain of driving and the
problems of parking. Everyone can enjoy the view and linear walks
become possible as there is no need to return to the car at the end of the
day. Fewer cars on the roads will make this lovely area a pleasanter place
for everyone to enjoy.

In the Torbay area Stagecoach Devon operates local services which
include rover tickets for use throughout the Torbay area. Open-top buses
run along the routes in the sea front area and by taking the bus to
Paignton Zoo visitors receive a discount on admission. Combined tickets
are available for journeys using the Paignton to Kingswear Steam Railway,
the Dartmouth Ferry, a cruise from Dartmouth to Totnes and return from
Totnes by bus. Contact Stagecoach Devon, ☎ 01803 613226 or enquire at
the Tourist Information Centres for more details.

Fact File

First Western National operate services throughout South Devon. Enquiries ☎ 01752 222666.

There are regular interlinking bus services to and across Dartmoor. Trains run along the Exeter to Plymouth line, the Tamar Valley line and on Sundays the Exeter to Okehampton line. These give access to towns on the edge of Dartmoor and, by connecting buses, to areas further afield. Anyone joining a Dartmoor National Park Guided Walk who arrives by public transport will not have to pay a fee for the walk.

The Dartmoor Public Transport Guide (published late May), available from National Park Information Centres gives all details or contact the Devon Bus Enquiry Line ☎ (01392), (01803) or (01271) 382800.

Plymouth Citybus operate The Discoverer, a regular circular service round the City which connects the railway station with the main tourist attractions. Day tickets enable unlimited travel round the city for the day, visiting as many attractions as possible in the time. Combined rail/ Discoverer tickets available from all stations in the region.
☎ 01752 222221 for details.

SWIMMING POOLS (INDOOR)

Brixham Pool, Higher Ranscombe Road,	☎ 01803 857151
Ivybridge - South Dartmoor Leisure Centre, Leonards Road,	☎ 01752 896999
Kingsbridge - Quayside Leisure Centre, Rope Walk,	☎ 01548 857100
Paignton - Torbay Leisure Centre,	☎ 01803 522240
Plymouth - Central Park Leisure Pools,	☎ 01752 560436
Plymouth - Seaton Pool	☎ 01752 778355
Plymouth Pavilions,	☎ 01752 222200
Plympton Pool,	☎ 01752 348459
Tavistock - Meadowlands Leisure Pool,	☎ 01822 617774
Torquay - Riviera Centre, Chestnut Avenue,	☎ 01803 299992
Torquay - Swim Torquay, Plainmoor,	☎ 01803 323400

TOURIST INFORMATION CENTRES

Those Centres marked with (✻) are open in the summer only.

Bovey Tracey, Station Road,	☎ 016263 832047
Brixham, Harbourside,	☎ 01803 852861
Dartmouth, Mayors Avenue,	☎ 01803 834224
Dawlish, The Lawn,	☎ 01626 863589
Exeter, Civic Centre,	☎ 01392 265700
Ivybridge, Leonards Road,	☎ 01752 897035
Kingsbridge, The Quay,	☎ 01548 853195
✻ Moretonhampstead, The Square,	☎ 01647 440043
Newton Abbot, Bridge House,	☎ 01626 367494

✳ Okehampton, West Street,   ☎ 01837 53020
Paignton, The Esplanade,   ☎ 01803 558383
Princetown, High Moorland Visitor Centre, ☎ 01822 890414
Plymouth, Island House, The Barbican,   ☎ 01752 264849
Salcombe, Market Street,   ☎ 01548 843927
✳ Tavistock, Bedford Square,   ☎ 01822 612938
Teignmouth, Seafront,   ☎ 01626 779769
Torquay, Vaughan Parade,   ☎ 01803 297428
Totnes, The Plains,   ☎ 01803 863168

There are also Devon Tourist Information Centres at:

Exeter Services Area (M5 Services at J30)   ☎ 01392 437581
✳ Tiverton Services
(off M5 J27, nr Sampford Peverell)   ☎ 01884 821242

WALKING

There are a number of walking trails in the area. Contact Devon Tourist Information Centre, Exeter Services, Sidmouth Road, Exeter, EX2 7HF, ☎ 01392 437581, for a free leaflet *Now You're Really Walking* outlining the routes. More detailed itineraries for each route can be purchased from the same address and other Tourist Information Centres.

The South West Coast Path runs for part of its 600 mile length along the South Devon coast. The South West Way Association produces a guide to the route with details of accommodation, transport, ferries and tide tables. South West Way Association ☎ 01803 873061.

The author of this book has written the offical guide book to that part of the route which runs through South Devon, ***South West Coast Path: Falmouth to Exmouth***, Aurum Press , 1990, updated 1999.

WATERSPORTS

Sailing

Brixham Yacht Club, Overgang Road,   ☎ 01803 853332
Paignton Sailing Club, South Quay,   ☎ 01803 525817
Plymouth - Fort Bovisand Sailing Centre,   ☎ 01752 482882
Plymouth - Royal Western Yacht Club,
   Queen Anne's Battery,   ☎ 01752 660077
Salcombe - Island Cruising Club,
   Island Street,   ☎ 01548 843481
Salcombe Dinghy Sailing,   ☎ 07970 017321 or
    01548 842840

Torquay - International Sailing School,
Beacon Quay,   ☎ 01803 291849

Torquay - Royal Torbay Yacht Club,
Beacon Hill,   ☎ 01803 292006

Windsurfing

Torquay Windsurf Centre/School,
Victoria Road,   ☎ 01803 212411

General

Newton Abbot - Devon Windsurf
and Canoe Centre, Decoy Lake,   ☎ 01803 312049.
Windsurfing, canoeing, kayaking, surf skis.
Also walks and cycle trails, picnic and play areas.

Salcombe - Courtlands Watersports,   ☎ 01548 843451.
Sailing, windsurfing, kayaking and water skiing.

WEATHER

For 1 to 10 day forecasts for South Devon call Weatherline:
☎ (0891) 600256.

For coastal forecast for sailors use Marine Call: ☎ (0891) 500458.

INDEX

LANDMARK
Publishing Ltd ● ● ● ●

VISITORS GUIDES

* Practical guides for the independent traveller
* Written in the form of touring itineraries
* Full colour illustrations and maps
* Detailed Landmark FactFile of practical information
* Landmark Visitors Guides highlight all the interesting places you will want to see, so ensuring that you make the most of your visit

LANDMARK VISITORS GUIDE

Devon

NEW INN HOTEL

Brian Le Messurier

Landmark Publishing
Waterloo House, 12 Compton, Ashbourne, Derbyshire DE6 IDA England
Tel: 01335 347349 Fax: 01335 347303 e-mail: landmark@clara.net
Catalogue sent on request

Published by
Landmark Publishing Ltd,
Waterloo House, 12 Compton, Ashbourne, Derbyshire DE6 1DA England
Tel: 01335 347349 Fax: 01335 347303 e-mail: landmark@clara.net

1st Edition
ISBN 1 901 522 52 0

© **Brian Le Messurier 1999**

The right of Brian Le Messurier as author of this work has been asserted by him
in accordance with the Copyright, Design and Patents Act, 1993.

All rights reserved. No part of this publication may be reproduced, stored in a
retrieval system or transmitted in any form or by any means, electronic,
mechanical, photocopying, recording or otherwise without the prior permission
of Landmark Publishing Ltd.

British Library Cataloguing in Publication Data: a catalogue record for this book
is available from the British Library.

Print: UIC Printing & Packaging Pte Ltd, Singapore
Cartography: Samantha Witham
Design: James Allsopp & Samantha Witham
Editor: Kay Coulson

Cover Pictures:

Front Cover: Morning sun brightens up the harbour at Brixham
Back cover, top: Fishing from the harbour wall at Dartmouth
Back cover, bottom: The 15th Century Cleave Inn at Lustleigh

Picture Credits:

Exeter City Council: Page 15, 19T & 19B
Powderham Castle, Exeter: Page 22
Devon County Council: Page 28B & 50
Keith Taylor: Page 25 & 28T
All other slides: Lindsey Porter

DISCLAIMER

While every care has been taken to ensure that the information in this book
is as accurate as possible at the time of publication, but the publishers
and author accept no responsibility for any loss, injury or inconvenience
sustained by anyone using this book.